Foul Deeds & Suspicious Deaths In & Around Southampton

TRUE CRIME FROM WHARNCLIFFE

Foul Deeds and Suspicious Deaths Series

Barking, Dagenham & Chadwell Heath
Barnsley
Bath
Bedford
Birmingham
Black Country
Blackburn and Hyndburn
Bolton
Bradford
Brighton
Bristol
Cambridge
Carlisle
Chesterfield
Colchester
Coventry
Croydon
Derby
Dublin
Durham
Ealing
Folkestone and Dover
Grimsby
Guernsey
Guildford
Halifax
Hampstead, Holborn and St Pancras
Huddersfield
Hull

Leeds
Leicester
Lewisham and Deptford
Liverpool
London's East End
London's West End
Manchester
Mansfield
More Foul Deeds Birmingham
More Foul Deeds Chesterfield
More Foul Deeds Wakefield
Newcastle
Newport
Norfolk
Northampton
Nottingham
Oxfordshire
Pontefract and Castleford
Portsmouth
Rotherham
Scunthorpe
Southend-on-Sea
Staffordshire and The Potteries
Stratford and South Warwickshire
Tees
Warwickshire
Wigan
York

OTHER TRUE CRIME BOOKS FROM WHARNCLIFFE

A-Z of Yorkshire Murder
Black Barnsley
Brighton Crime and Vice 1800-2000
Durham Executions
Essex Murders
Executions & Hangings in Newcastle
and Morpeth
Norfolk Mayhem and Murder

Norwich Murders
Strangeways Hanged
The A-Z of London Murders
Unsolved Murders in Victorian and
Edwardian London
Unsolved Norfolk Murders
Unsolved Yorkshire Murders
Yorkshire's Murderous Women

Please contact us via any of the methods below for more information or a catalogue.

WHARNCLIFFE BOOKS

47 Church Street – Barnsley – South Yorkshire – S70 2AS
Tel: 01226 734555 – 734222 Fax: 01226 – 734438
E-mail: enquiries@pen-and-sword.co.uk
Website: www.wharncliffebooks.co.uk

Foul Deeds & Suspicious Deaths In & Around

SOUTHAMPTON

JOHN J EDDLESTON

First Published in Great Britain in 2009 by
Wharncliffe Books
an imprint of
Pen and Sword Books Ltd.
47 Church Street
Barnsley
South Yorkshire
S70 2AS

Copyright © John J Eddleston 2009

ISBN: 978-1-84563-097-3

Typeset in 11/13pt Plantin by Concept, Huddersfield.

Printed and bound in England by
CPI UK.

Pen & Sword Books Ltd incorporates the Imprints of Pen
& Sword Aviation, Pen & Sword Maritime, Pen & Sword
Military, Wharncliffe Local History, Pen & Sword Select,
Pen & Sword Military Classics, Leo Cooper, Remember
When, Seaforth Publishing and Frontline Publishing.

For a complete list of Pen & Sword titles please contact
PEN & SWORD BOOKS LIMITED
47 Church Street
Barnsley
South Yorkshire
S70 2BR
England
E-mail: enquiries@pen-and-sword.co.uk
Website: www.pen-and-sword.co.uk

Contents

Acknowledgements

I would like to offer my thanks to a number of people who greatly assisted in the preparation of this volume.

First and foremost I would like to thank my wife, Yvonne. Not only did she help with the research, making copious notes for me, but also proof read every story.

I would also like to thank the staff of The National Archives at Kew and the staff of the British Newspaper Library at Colindale in London.

Finally I would like to thank the publishers, Pen and Sword books, and especially Mr Rupert Harding.

Thank you one and all.

Chapter 1

The Navvy
James Caffyn
1877

John Barber, who lived at Elmfield, near Ryde, on
the Isle of Wight, hadn't seen his daughter Maria
in something approaching thirteen years. Then,
suddenly, in the autumn of 1877, she appeared on his doorstep
with a man in tow. Maria introduced the man as her boyfriend
and gave his name as James Caffyn.

Jim, as everyone knew Caffyn, was working on the railway
and on some reclamation works, at St Helens. He had actually
been living with Maria for some eight or nine months, having
first met her when they shared lodgings at Clifton Villas in
Brighton. From there they had moved on to Hastings before
Maria had expressed a desire to see some old friends and her
family back on the Isle of Wight. It was for that reason that the
couple, accompanied by their little black and white dog, had
travelled to the island.

The couple seemed to be quite happy in each other's company and a somewhat understanding John invited the couple
into his home and offered them the upstairs room where they
could live together. Meanwhile, the lower rooms continued to
be occupied by John Barber and his common-law wife, Caroline
Brown. For some weeks, all was well.

On Monday, 26 November, all four occupants of the house
enjoyed breakfast together before John and Mrs Brown went
off to their work, leaving Caffyn and Maria alone. At around
10.15am that same morning, Hugh Benjamin Grist, who ran a
greengrocer's shop from the house next door, was outside his
premises when a rather excited Maria Barber ran up to him and
cried: 'For God's sake come in, for he has pinched me, kicked
me and tried to strangle me.'

Mr Grist followed Maria back into John Barber's house and there saw the man he recognised as Jim. The two men had not really spoken much to each other in the past but Jim had called into the shop once or twice. Now, Jim was swearing loudly and all of his profanities were directed towards Maria. Hugh asked him what the matter was but Jim did not reply and merely asked Maria for his clothes. She immediately went upstairs and returned a minute or so later with a pile of clothes which she handed over to Jim adding, for good measure: 'I'll give you all the money I've got if you'll go.'

Again, Jim did not reply but left the room and went upstairs himself. He too soon returned, carrying two short whips, a dog's chain and an axe. He placed the axe on the floor and the other items on a wooden table in the centre of the room. Throughout all this, the little dog he and Maria had brought to the island, lay in its bed in the corner of the room. Jim glanced at the animal and said that it belonged to him and he would take it with him, Maria immediately replied that he should not have it. Jim, however, did not rise to this bait. The couple now appeared to be quiet again so Hugh Grist left them alone. After all, this domestic dispute was not really any of his business.

At some time after 4.00pm, Caroline Brown and John Barber returned home. Whilst John put the pony and trap away, Caroline entered the house, only to run screaming from it moments later. Once again, it was Hugh Grist who was asked for assistance. He timed Caroline's appeal for assistance at around 4.10pm or a little later.

Going into Barber's house again, Hugh Grist saw that Maria lay in the corner of the downstairs room, in a pool of blood. Her head had almost been hacked from her body and the axe Hugh had seen earlier lay a short distance from her feet. Even as Hugh Grist surveyed this terrible scene, John Barber entered, picked up the axe and laid it against the fender of the fireplace. Then, as he stayed to comfort Caroline Brown, Grist ran to fetch the local police officer, Sergeant Daniels.

It was around 5.00pm when Sergeant James Daniels returned to the house with Hugh Grist. He noticed that Maria's head and shoulders were resting on the dog's bed, which was now heavily bloodstained. The dog itself was on its lead but had been unable to escape the room as the other end of the lead was trapped underneath Maria's body. Sergeant Daniels also noted a severe wound on the left side of Maria's forehead and another in her neck. Though it was obvious that Maria Barber was beyond all human aid, she would still have to be examined by a medical practitioner and, once again, it was Hugh Grist who was sent for help.

Of Jim, or James Caffyn, there was no sign. It was surmised that, seeking to escape, he had almost certainly left the island and enquiries soon showed that a man matching his description had caught the 1.00pm boat to Southsea. A description of Caffyn was now circulated on the mainland and this led to the arrest of a man in the *Victoria Tavern*, in Queen Street, Portsea, by Constable James Thomas, on the following morning. The man was interviewed by Inspector Hood but denied that his name was James Caffyn. Later that same day, Sergeant Daniels travelled to Portsea from the Isle of Wight and made a positive identification. Caffyn was then escorted back to the island. Once there, another identification was made by John Barber and Caffyn was then charged with wilful murder.

In due course, Caffyn appeared before the magistrates where he was remanded but after the hearing he made a full statement to the officer who had charge of him. In this, he freely admitted that he was responsible for Maria's death. The statement began: 'Last Monday morning we had a few words, not many; not so many as has been represented; and I was determined that she should deceive no more men as long as she lived.'

'After I said that I deliberately took that axe off the table. I delivered one blow on the forehead with the face of the axe, and knocked her down to where she was lying. The first blow I hit her with the face of the axe. Then I hit her on the cheek.'

'The next blow I delivered across the throat. That was all the blows she had; only three and there is one thing I did not state to you sir. We drinked [sic] a pint of beer between us before I committed the deed. That is the deed, sir.'

'I done it with a good heart and now I am willing to die the same. If I had my will, no man and woman should be allowed to cohabit together, for that is the cause of all the murders and I hope you will make it public to the country.'

Caffyn's trial took place on 22 January 1878, before Mister Justice Mellor, with the case for his defence resting in the hands of Mr Charles Matthews. The case for the prosecution was led by Mr Werry who was assisted by Mr Temple Cooke.

There could be no doubt that Caffyn was responsible for Maria's death but could the charge be reduced to one of manslaughter? Much was made of Maria Barber's past. Apparently, during the thirteen years since her father had last seen her, she had been married and left her husband once she had tired of him. There had followed a number of relationships during which Maria would find a new man, spend a few weeks with him and then leave him. Unfortunately for her, when she had tried to do the same with James Caffyn, he had retaliated and killed her. Surely his attack upon her had been caused by such a degree of aggravation that the charge should be reduced to one of manslaughter.

In the event, the jury took just a few minutes to decide that this was a case of murder and Caffyn was guilty as charged. Caffyn was duly condemned to death and that sentence was carried out at Winchester, on Monday, 11 February 1878 by William Marwood. It was reported that Caffyn walked bravely to the scaffold. Once the trap had been sprung, he struggled for some two minutes at the end of the rope whilst his heart continued to beat for up to ten long minutes. Caffyn was the last man to be hanged for a crime committed on the Isle of Wight.

Chapter 2

The Best of Friends Albert Edward Brown 1886

On Tuesday, 23 March 1886, Frederick Roberts, the master of the ship *Nellie*, welcomed aboard a young man who identified himself as Edward Brown. After some discussion, Roberts signed Brown on as an ordinary seaman and explained that the ship was due to leave harbour on the 28th, and head for Southampton.

Two days after this, on 25 March, another man, eighteen-year-old James Stanley Parker, also joined the ship and, almost from the outset, he and Brown became firm friends.

The *Nellie* did indeed leave Greenwich on 28 March and only arrived in Southampton at noon on Saturday, 3 April. It had been a very bad voyage for Parker who had suffered badly from sea-sickness. Fortunately for him, his new friend, Brown had done much of his work for him and this only served to cement the relationship between the two men.

The ship's cargo was unloaded the following Monday and Tuesday and it was on this final day, 6 April, that Frederick Roberts paid off both Brown and Parker. Parker was paid four shillings and Brown, by far the more experienced man, was paid seventeen shillings and six pence. There was, however, one final matter to sort out. Roberts knew that Brown had borrowed a shilling from Parker whilst they were still in London and another when they had landed at Southampton. This led to a minor disagreement, Brown claiming that he only owed his friend a shilling whilst Parker maintained that it was two. Frederick Roberts intervened and ordered Brown to pay over two shillings, which he did, without argument. The two men left the ship together, at noon the next day, Wednesday, 7 April and set off to walk back to London.

Not long after this, the two men were seen entering the High Street by Constable Bernard Camerford who couldn't help but notice Brown's bright yellow oilskin. The constable noticed that both men were carrying bundles, the older man's, Brown's, being the larger of the two.

Some minutes later, Edward Dudley Jeffries, a porter at Southampton railway station, took a bundle from James Parker who paid sixpence for carriage to London. It was now some time between 1.00pm and 2.00pm.

The night of 7 April was an extremely wet one and the weather seemed to be unrelenting. No doubt it was with some relief that Brown and Parker sought refuge in the *Hyde Tavern* at around 6.30pm where Emily Sophia Mitchell served them both with a pint of three-penny beer. They left at around 6.45pm whilst it was still raining heavily.

The next sighting of the friends was made at 7.00pm that same night. Edward Norris, a gardener, left Toll Gate Cottage, heading for Winchester when he passed two men close to the mile stone. The younger man asked Norris if they were on the right road for London and was pleased to be told that they

High Street, Southampton as it looked at the time Constable Camerford saw Albert Brown walking with James Parker, the man he would murder later that same day.

were. Norris noticed that the other man, dressed in a yellow oilskin, carried a large bag over his shoulder.

Moments after this, Jonathan Bedford also drove past the two men, heading up Barton Hill. He too remembered the yellow oilskin and the large bundle thrown over one shoulder.

Henry Piper was a farm labourer and on Friday, 9 April, he was sent to fetch a horse-drill. He walked to a farm owned by Mr W R Simonds and was told that the drill was in a field. Going to the location, Piper found the drill but the shafts appeared to be missing. He noticed that there was a good deal of straw scattered around, possibly due to the awful weather they had had of late, and thought that the shafts might be hidden underneath. However, as Piper drew nearer to one of the hay-ricks, he could see that there was something underneath the straw, which certainly was not the missing shafts. Piper walked closer still and then, some two yards or so from one of the ricks, Piper saw a man's arm and head poking out beneath the straw.

Piper immediately reported his find to Alfred Taylor a farmer and blacksmith. He in turn passed the information on to Constable Joseph Gladwell but it was perhaps 5.30pm before the officer, in the company of Constable William Smith, arrived at the field, to find that there were several small boys standing by the gate, not wanting to miss anything that transpired in the field.

The two policemen made a careful search of the body and the surrounding area. Constable Gladwell found two hand-kerchiefs, a scarf, a pair of gloves and a knife. Some five yards from the body lay a cap, also partly hidden beneath some straw. The young man, whoever he was, lay on his back and there was a good deal of blood around his head. It looked like he had been battered before his throat had been cut. When that search was widened somewhat, a razor and a hammer were found hidden underneath a hedge in the lane nearby.

On Sunday, 11 April, Dr William A Richards conducted a post-mortem on the dead man. He reported that there were three separate wounds on the head, suggesting three blows. Two of these were on the top of the head and one on the temple. None of these had caused any serious injury but would have stunned the man. There was a single wound in the throat, caused by a very sharp instrument and this had been the direct cause of death. The knife found on the dead man bore no traces of blood so had not been used in the attack.

Dr Richards was also able to give the opinion that the throat wound had been caused whilst the man was lying on the ground. The suggestion was that the three blows had rendered him unconscious or at least dazed him and then the cut to the throat had been inflicted whilst he was helpless.

Reports of the crime and a description of the man led Henry Parker to come forward on 12 April to identify the body as that of his son, James. He told officers that James had turned eighteen last December and he had last seen his son on 25 March when he had said that he was going to join the crew of the *Nellie*, docked at Greenwich. This led officers to interview the ship's master, Frederick Roberts, who told them of the friendship with Brown and the fact that the two men had left Southampton together, intending to travel back to London. It was now time to interview that companion whose full name was actually Albert Edward Brown.

It wasn't long before Brown was traced to his home in Deptford. Sergeant William Morgan called at the house at 12.15am on 11 April and asked him about Parker. Brown readily admitted that they had started walking back to London together but close to Winchester they had parted company. They had met a man and a woman who fell into conversation with them and they had said that they were on their way to London and would take Parker with them. Brown had then shaken hands with Parker and said goodbye. This failed to explain why Parker had decided to travel alone and, not satisfied with the explanation, Sergeant Morgan took Brown to the police station for further questioning.

Arrested and charged with murder, Brown appeared before Mister Justice Day at Winchester on 10 May. During the two day trial, Brown was defended by Mr W Lopes whilst the case for the prosecution was led by Mr Charles Matthews who was assisted by Mr W Box.

Further evidence of the friendly relationship that had existed between Brown and James Parker was given by Southampton dock workers who had helped unload the *Nellie*.

Charles Tuffin had gone on board the ship on Saturday, 3 April. He had returned on the 7th and on that date had heard Brown and Parker say that they intended to walk to London. Indeed, Brown had said that he would look after Parker and see him all the way into the capital.

John Lawrence had been another seaman who had helped unload and after the two men had been paid off, he helped both Brown and Parker to pack their bags. At one stage he had seen Brown pack two razors in his large bag. This had taken place at around 10.00am, on 7 April.

The master of the *Nellie*, Mr Roberts, had seen much of the two men on the voyage from Greenwich. He confirmed the friendly relationship that had existed between them. However, he was able to add that he knew that Brown had amongst his possessions a hammer, a chisel, a gimlet and a large sheath knife. He also confirmed that there were only four men on the ship during the voyage.

The fourth man had been David Owens, the ship's mate. He too knew that Brown had the hammer, chisel, gimlet and knife and during the journey, Brown had mentioned to him that he had plenty of razors. He also confirmed that Brown was trying to borrow money once they had docked in Southampton. Brown had asked him for a loan of sixpence or, if he couldn't manage that, fourpence, to pay for his trip back to London. Owens refused to lend him any money.

Witnesses had already come forward to confirm that the two men started the journey to London together but now other testimony showed that from 8 April onwards, Brown was on his own.

Benjamin Smith and Richard Mott had set out together, from Winchester, at around 4.00am on 8 April. Close to Barton Hill they saw a man standing alone at the gate to a field which had two hayricks. By then it was 4.45am and the man they had seen was Brown.

Frederick Shergold, a carman, left his home at 5.00am. At 5.20am he passed a man heading in the opposite direction. He had since positively identified that man as Brown and confirmed that he was alone.

Another witness who had seen Brown was Joseph Glaespool, a milk-seller, who left his home in Winchester at 5.10am on

8 April. He had seen Brown close to Warner's Lodge and noticed that he had something in his left hand, which he was brushing down with his right. It looked like a brown coat or mackintosh and as Glaespool drew nearer, Brown stuffed the garment into his bag. The two men exchanged a cheery 'Good Morning' and Brown then asked if he was on the right road for the railway station.

By 5.45am, Brown had arrived at Winchester railway station for he was seen by Charles Bartlett, the foreman porter. Another porter, William Brothers, also saw Brown who asked him which was the train to Woking. A third railway employee, Harry Roe saw Brown again at 7.23am when he asked if a train standing at the platform was for Woking. Brothers confirmed that it was and advised Brown to jump on.

It could be proved that Brown had travelled by train as far as Woking for Arthur Cox, the booking clerk at Winchester, had been asked by Brown how far he could go for three shillings and six pence. Cox told him that that amount of money would take him to Woking and Brown then purchased a ticket.

Eventually, Brown had arrived at his father-in-law's house in Greenwich. Charles Edward Delatouche testified that Brown had arrived at around 8.30pm on 8 April. Brown said he had walked some thirty miles and was very tired. Soon afterwards, Brown's wife had come in and asked him for some money. Brown had jokingly said that he hadn't got any but then handed over ten shillings in silver.

Charles' wife, Sarah Ann, confirmed this story but also added that Brown had spoken several times about a mate of his who he had walked home with. He said he had felt sorry for him as he had been very sick whilst they were at sea.

Having heard all the evidence, the jury had little difficulty in returning a guilty verdict and Brown was duly sentenced to death. He was then sent to Winchester prison to await his fate. It was whilst Brown was in the condemned cell that he made a full confession to the crime.

On 13 May, Brown made a statement saying that by the time he left Southampton he only had just over ten shillings in cash upon him and he knew that he would have even less when he got home. It clearly wasn't enough to hand over to his wife so he decided that he would rob his friend, somewhere along the road.

The weather was very bad but the two men decided that they would try to get at least some sleep in the field. Brown decided that this would be a good place to steal Parker's money and his intention was to knock him out using the hammer he had in his bag, take the cash and then be on his way.

It was about 4.00am and Parker said he wanted to move to the other side of the hayrick as water was dripping off, onto his head. Brown took the opportunity to take out the hammer but he thought better of his plan and was about to put it away again when something came over him. He lashed out at Parker, striking him on the head but the blow did not stun him and he began to cry out. So loud were his screams that Brown had to hit him twice more. Then, afraid that the noise would attract someone's attention, Brown took out one of his razors and cut Parker's throat. Once Parker was dead, Brown helped himself to four shillings and six pence in silver, two half-pennies and a bronze farthing.

Having taken the money, Brown then took off his oilskin and put it inside his bag. He placed the razor and the hammer underneath a hedge close to the gate and headed off for Winchester. He confirmed his railway journey to Woking and then hitched a ride on a cart to London Bridge before going on to Deptford. He ended by saying that there had been no intention to kill Parker and he had not known what had come over him.

On 25 May, a final attempt was made to save Brown's life. Mr Joseph Bell, a gentleman who knew the family well, forwarded evidence that as a child, Brown had fallen from a third storey window and badly injured himself. He had suffered a bad head injury and there was a suggestion that he had never been in his right mind since that time. Examples of his bizarre behaviour were given including that whilst at sea, he had been known to strip himself naked and sleep on deck underneath the sails.

None of this served to save Brown. After the jury had been out for just over an hour, they returned to announce that Brown was guilty. As a result, on 31 May, he was hanged at Winchester alongside James Whelan who had killed George Richardson, on board a ship at sea and thrown his body overboard. It was reported that whilst he stood on the trap, waiting to be launched into eternity, Brown had cried out: 'Lord Jesus, have mercy on my soul.

Chapter 3

Circumstantial Evidence
Frederick Burden
1896

Towards the end of 1880, Angelina Stainer, the daughter of a brothel-keeper, married Alfred John Faithful, a seaman, and moved into 29 Mount Street, Southampton. By the census of 1891, the family, now also including an eight-year-old daughter Ethel and a five-year-old son, Alfred, had moved to 14 Wharf Street. Some two years after this, on 14 December 1893, Angelina walked out on her family and began earning her living as a prostitute.

Very soon after she had left her husband, Angelina became friendly with Annie Nicholls who lived at 16 Brooklyn Road, Portswood. At one stage, Angelina even lived with Annie's mother, who also had a house in Brooklyn Road, but then, early in 1896, Angelina moved further along the same street, into number 9. By then she had met Frederick Burden and they had started living together. Unfortunately, there were constant arguments between the couple and in due course, Frederick moved out, though he was still a regular visitor to the house.

Eleven-year-old Sarah Matilda Philpott was yet another resident of Brooklyn Road, residing at number 14. Sarah had become quite friendly with Angelina and would often run errands for her. At around 1.00pm on Thursday, 20 February 1896, young Sarah called at number 9, to see if Angelina needed anything. She knocked, but there was no reply. Luckily, she had a front door key which Angelina had given to Annie Nicholls and which she, in turn, had passed on to Sarah.

Sarah took out the key but for some reason it would not turn in the lock. Not one to be deterred, Sarah ran around to the back door, which she found was unlocked. She entered the house and called out for Angelina but again there was no reply.

Going upstairs, Sarah entered the front bedroom and saw Angelina lying in bed, with a great deal of blood about her face. Sarah touched nothing but immediately ran to get help.

Sarah had run home to tell her mother what she had found. Mrs Philpott then ran to number 15, a house occupied by Charles Murray and his family. Charles listened to the story of what Sarah had found and then went to Angelina's house to investigate for himself. He too was unable to gain access through the front door and went around the back. Inside Angelina's bedroom he saw the scene for himself and, disturbing nothing, went for the police.

Inspector Henry Hurst was the first police officer on the scene and it was he who sent for Doctor Ives. Meanwhile, Hurst made a careful inspection of the premises. The bedroom in which the body was found was the only furnished room in the entire house. It contained a chair, a dressing table, a bed, a fender, the frame of a sewing machine, a basket which stood near the bed, a hearthrug and a carpet, all of which were of poor quality.

Angelina was lying on her left side, facing the window. Her throat had been cut so badly that her head was almost severed from her body. A bloodstained razor, presumably the weapon used, lay loosely in Angelina's right hand between her extended thumb and forefinger. The body was fully clothed, apart from boots and an apron lay underneath the neck. By the side of the bed, in the basket, lay a bodice, spotted with blood. There was a towel lying alongside the body and a sheet underneath. The pillow beneath Angelina's head was very heavily bloodstained but two other pillows, on one side of the body, only bore a few spots of blood. A bucket to one side of the bed contained some water, which was mixed with blood. Finally, Inspector Hurst noted that an oil-lamp was still burning in the room.

The fact that the razor was found in Angelina's hand might have suggested that she had taken her own life but when Doctor William Robert Yeates Ives made his initial examination, he stated that the wound could not possibly be self-inflicted. This was a case of murder and the killer, whoever he or she was, had tried to make it look like a suicide. It was time to find out who Angelina had been close to and, once the neighbours were interviewed, Inspector Hurst found that one name was repeated again and again; that of Frederick Burden.

It soon transpired that the last person to see Angelina alive had been Sarah Matilda Philpott, the same young girl who had found the body. Sarah had called on Angelina at around 5.00pm on Wednesday, 19 February. It was Sarah's habit to light the fire for Angelina most evenings but on this occasion she found that it was already burning. At the time, both Angelina and Burden were in the house. They were arguing and Sarah reported that she believed that Angelina was drunk.

After some time, there was a knock on the front door and Burden went to answer it. He returned to say to Sarah that her father wanted her but she ignored this and stayed. Some time later there was a second knock and this time, everyone ignored it and the caller went away. At around 7.00pm, Sarah left and found her sister, Jane, waiting for her outside. The two girls went home together. This was the last time anyone would ever see Angelina alive. The police were now sure that Angelina Faithfull had been killed at some time between 7.00pm on 19 February and 1.00pm on the 20th.

Annie Nicholls had much information to give to the police. The first incident she referred to had taken place on 1 February of that year. She had gone across to Angelina's house to find her with Burden. Angelina was lying on her bed, gasping for breath and couldn't speak. Annie assumed that Burden had hit Angelina or hurt her in some other way and told him to fetch the doctor. He had merely replied that he had no money to pay for a doctor. At that point Annie left the house but returned later to ask Angelina what had happened. Angelina told her that she had argued with Burden and told him she was going to leave. He had said that if she left, she would leave without a limb.

Another incident had taken place on 16 February, just a few days before Angelina had been killed. Once again, Annie had found them both in the bedroom and upon seeing her friend, Angelina complained that Burden had tried to strangle her. As if to prove this, she showed Annie some red marks upon her neck. Angelina also said that she believed Burden had poisoned some beer that was in a jug. Hearing this, Burden had poured himself two and a half tumblers of the brew and quickly drank it down. However, Annie was able to report that he had then left the room and gone into a back room. Annie had heard the sounds of a window being opened, followed by the sounds of retching and vomiting and when Burden returned a few moments later, he was wiping his mouth. Did this mean that the beer had been poisoned after all?

Soon after this incident, Annie had asked Angelina to go to the *Brook Inn* for a drink. Burden had gone too and after having yet another glass of beer he went outside the pub. He was back inside a minute and volunteered the information that he had just been sick. The three only stayed in the pub for some eight minutes and as they left, Burden kissed Angelina and bade her goodnight, adding: 'I shall not trouble you anymore.' Finally, Annie was able to say that she had seen Burden twice the next day, 17 February, but had not seen him since.

It was now crucial for the police to speak to Frederick Burden but he had gone missing from his father's house at 168 Middle Street, Kingsland Drive. Further, there was evidence that he had suddenly walked away from his work.

Burden was employed by the Union Company, on the docks, and his immediate boss was John Barton. Barton told the police that Burden had reported for work at 7.00am on 19 February, but at 8.30am, he had been seen leaving the ship he was working on and had not returned to his post. Burden was supposed to work until 5.00pm.

In due course it came to the attention of the police that Burden had indeed returned to his father's house. So it was that at 9.15pm on Saturday, 22 February, Detective Sergeant John William Boggeln and Detective Hatcher called at the house in Middle Street to question him. Burden was in a back room and immediately the police officers noticed that he had an injury to his throat. Asked about the death of Angelina faithfull, Burden made a full statement, which was taken down in writing.

Burden began: 'I am not guilty. I was on the bridge at Winchester, near the barracks, at nine o'clock on Thursday morning. I then went to Romsey where I slept under a hayrick and I went on to Salisbury where I saw, on a placard, 'A Sad Fate of a Woman in Southampton'.

'I came back to Romsey and had a pint of beer at the *Sun* and asked the landlord for a paper. I then read the full account and came back to Southampton where I intended to give myself up.'

Burden was then escorted to the police station where he was formally charged with murder, his only reply being: 'I suppose it looks pretty black against me.' He was then searched and Boggeln found a dock labourer's work ticket for 19 February. His clothes were taken and handed to Dr Ives for examination and Burden was then taken to Winchester prison where he would be held prior to appearing in court.

Frederick Burden's trial opened at Winchester before Mister Justice Day on 29 June 1896. The case for the prosecution was led by Mr C T Giles and Mr Barnes whilst Burden was defended by Mr E H Bullen.

The court opened at 10.00am and there was a rather undignified rush for spaces in the public gallery, which was soon filled, leaving many would-be spectators outside the room. Burden appeared soon after 10.25am and, asked how he wished to plead, answered 'Not Guilty' in a strong voice.

In his opening speech for the prosecution, Mr Giles detailed the wounds inflicted upon Angelina stating that the cut in her throat ran from ear to ear and was so deep that even the bones in the neck had been severed. There was blood upon the handle of the razor found loosely held in Angelina's hand but none upon the hand itself. This indicated that the wound must have been inflicted by someone else. Mr Giles then began to call his witnesses.

One of the first of those witnesses was Sarah Philpott. She gave her evidence in a very quiet voice and the judge complained that he couldn't hear what she said. Sarah was asked to speak up. After outlining what she had already told the police, Sarah agreed, under cross-examination, that she had seen other men besides Burden calling at Angelina's house but added that this hadn't happened very often.

Dr Ives, the police surgeon for the district, gave full details of the injuries Angelina had suffered. The wound in the throat began one and a half inches below the lobe of the right ear and ran across to a point two and a half inches below the left lobe.

In the doctor's opinion, according to his initial examination, Angelina had been dead between twelve and fourteen hours.

On Monday, 24 February, Dr Ives had conducted the post-mortem. In addition to the wound in the neck, Dr Ives had also seen a round bruise over the navel, some three and a half inches across. Angelina also had a black eye and death had been due to loss of blood, the body being almost drained.

Two days earlier, on 22 February, after Burden had been arrested, Dr Ives reported to the police station to make an examination of the prisoner. Burden had incised wounds to his neck. These were mainly superficial and were around two or perhaps three days old. Burden had claimed that he had sustained these when he fell onto a barbed wire fence at Romsey but Dr Ives did not think this could be the case as such wounds would almost certainly have been infected.

Turning to his examination of Burden's clothing, Dr Ives reported that there were bloodstains on the right hand sleeve of his coat and another large stain on the inside of the lining. There was blood around the collar of Burden's shirt and several spots on the sleeves. In addition, bloodstains were seen on his vest, though these were only small spots, and a single spot of blood had been found on Burden's drawers, on the left leg.

Dr Ives was able to give one final piece of interesting information. When Angelina's body had been found, the lamp was still burning in the bedroom. Tests had shown that this lamp would burn, assuming that the reservoir was full, for between twelve and fourteen hours. The body had been found at 1.00pm on 20 February suggesting that the very latest the lamp could have been lit would be 11.00pm the previous night, some four hours after Angelina had been seen in Burden's company. This fitted in with the testimony as to the time of death, placing it at some time between 11.00pm on 19 February and 1.00am on the 20th.

George Parton said that at some time between 7.00am and 9.00am, he had seen Burden some 500 yards away from the murder scene. Parton could not be sure of the exact date this encounter had taken place but he recalled that he had first heard of the murder that same evening. The inference was that this must have been on the day the body was discovered, Thursday,

20 February. This testimony was greatly devalued, however, when Parton said that he had heard of the murder at noon. Angelina's body was not found until 1.00pm. Further, Parton said that the man he had seen was heading towards Southampton, not away from it.

Stephen Paddick lived in Banner Street, Romsey and he testified that at around 7.00am on Friday, 21 February he was on his way to Squab Wood when he saw a man crossing a field, which contained two hayricks. The man got on to the Salisbury road and waited for Paddick to approach. The two men fell into conversation and the stranger asked for a light for his cigarette. Paddick positively identified the man as Burden and added that he had asked him if he had heard of a murder in Southampton. He went on to ask if he had seen the previous night's newspaper and then sought confirmation as to how long it would take him to get to Salisbury.

Much was made of this comment in Mr Giles' summation for the prosecution. He stated that it was well known that Burden had threatened Angelina. They had been together until at least 7.00pm on 19 February and there was no evidence that anyone else had argued with her after this time. Dr Ives had confirmed that Burden had come into contact with a good deal of blood and this did not seem to be accounted for by his own injuries. Mr Giles referred to Burden being seen 500 yards away from the house, early on 20 February, by George Parton, even though this evidence had largely been discounted and finally, he had spoken to Stephen Paddick about the murder in Southampton. How could he have known about it, unless he had committed it?

For the defence, it was confirmed that reports of the murder had appeared in the later editions of the *Southern Daily Echo* on 20 February. Burden claimed to have heard a news-vendor shouting out about the murder and had later read reports that showed he was being sought by the police. It was readily acknowledged that Burden had returned voluntarily to Southampton and this was hardly the action of a guilty man.

Turning to the previous incidents, mentioned by some of the witnesses, Mr Bullen said that there had indeed been frequent quarrels between his client and the dead woman. She had persuaded him to leave his family and live with her but had then continued to see other men. As for the supposed incident of the poisoned beer, Burden had already been drinking rather heavily and the two and a half tumblers of beer he then consumed so quickly, naturally made him sick. There was no proof that the beer had ever been poisoned. Finally, although the razor used to kill Angelina did indeed belong to Burden, he had left that at the house and so anyone could have picked it up and used it.

The jury retired at 3.00pm. Two hours later they returned to court to say that they could not agree on a verdict. The judge asked them to continue their deliberations but by 6.00pm, the foreman confirmed that it was impossible for them to agree, even if they had to stay together all night.

On 30 June, the day after the trial had concluded and the jury had been discharged, Mr Bullen was back in court asking the judge if it was his intention to try Burden again at this same assizes or order some future date. The problem was that many of the witnesses called were rather nomadic and there might be a good deal of difficulty in getting them all together again.

In the event, the second trial opened on 1 July. The same witnesses gave the same evidence and the second jury retired to decide on the guilt or innocence of the prisoner. After a deliberation of some twenty-five minutes they returned to announce that Burden was guilty, though they did add a recommendation to mercy on account of the prisoner's age. Asked if he had anything to say before the sentence of death was passed, Burden replied: 'All I can say is that I did not do it.'

There was to be no reprieve. Despite the fact that all the evidence was circumstantial, that one jury had failed to agree and that the second had recommended him to mercy, twenty-four-year-old Frederick Burden was hanged at Winchester on Thursday, 16 July 1896. In fact, this was a triple execution, Burden being hanged alongside Samuel Edward Smith, a soldier who had killed a corporal at Aldershot and Philip Matthews, who had murdered his daughter at Teignmouth. It was the last ever triple execution in England.

In the days before he died on the gallows, Burden had been visited several times by his father. His mother, however, showed a much more callous attitude. Whilst it was true that she maintained that her son was innocent, she did not visit him once in prison and, on the day following the execution, had a friend write to the governor of the prison asking for the death certificate, so that she would be able to claim a £25 insurance policy on Frederick's life.

Chapter 4

Ruled by the Moon
Charles Maidment
1899

Charles Maidment was in love and the object of his affection, eighteen year old Dorcas Houghton, seemed to return that love. By the spring of 1899, the couple, who both lived in Sarisbury, had been seeing each other for some two years but then, on Tuesday, 18 April of that year, Dorcas dropped a bombshell on twenty-two year old Maidment.

Dorcas and Maidment met by arrangement early on the evening of 18 April and she informed him that she didn't want their relationship to continue any longer. She would not walk out with him anymore and would see him the following evening so that she could return the presents he had given her. Charles tried to persuade Dorcas to stay with him, but she was not to be moved.

The presents Dorcas referred to were actually of little import. They consisted of nothing more than two handkerchiefs and a card Maidment had given to her the previous Christmas, written in affectionate terms. Maidment, however, suspected what was behind all this. Dorcas had mentioned another young man she had met, a marine artilleryman who was due to return home in May after serving his country overseas. It was obvious to the grief-stricken young man that Dorcas preferred the marine to him and would soon be walking out with him instead. A saddened Charles Maidment returned home that evening and brooded on his position, having arranged to meet Dorcas in Swanwick Lane the next day.

At 6.00pm on Wednesday, 19 April 1899, Dorcas left her home. She was seen going out by her mother, Augusta, who noticed that she was carrying two things: a book and a small brown-paper parcel. Augusta watched as Dorcas headed off towards Swanwick Lane. Augusta thought that perhaps she was going to visit her sister who lived over that way.

Henry Fielder was a letter-carrier or postman and part of his duties involved delivering mail in the area and emptying the postboxes each evening. It was for this latter reason that he walked past Manor Farm, to clear the box in Swanwick Lane. As Fielder strolled down the lane he noticed Maidment leaning over a gate near the farm. Maidment appeared to be in good spirits as he shouted: 'Good evening Mr Fielder,' and Henry returned the friendly greeting.

It was just as Henry Fielder was emptying the postbox that Dorcas came into view, walking down the lane towards where Maidment waited. Fielder saw that she carried a novel in her left hand, which she was reading as she walked. Underneath her arm, she carried a small parcel. Fielder nodded to her and continued with his duties.

The postbox was emptied and locked and Fielder turned to face up the lane, in the direction he had just come. As he turned he saw Dorcas and Maidment exchange a couple of words and then walk off together. In effect, Fielder was now following them up the hill.

The young couple were some distance in front of Fielder, with Maidment walking on the right side of his young lady. There was a curve in the road ahead and the couple vanished from Fielder's sight as they passed around that bend. Seconds later, a loud report rang out, shattering the quiet of the country lane.

Even as Fielder puzzled over what the noise might have been he saw Maidment running back towards him. Then, just as suddenly, Maidment changed direction and headed off over a field. Concerned that something might have happened to Dorcas, Fielder ran to the top of the hill and turned the curve in the lane. There, to his horror, he found Dorcas Houghton quite dead, a single bullet wound underneath her right ear. Further, there were clear signs of burning and scorching around the wound showing that the gun used to kill her must have been held quite close to her head.

The shot, heard by Fielder, had also been heard by others. Edward Knapp lived with his father in Swanwick Lane and was in a field adjoining the lane when he heard a loud bang. Turning in the direction the noise had come from, Edward saw Charles Maidment running across the field towards him. Edward knew Maidment well and shouted: 'Hello Charlie, what's up?' Maidment did not reply directly to the question but muttered something about needing to find the footpath. Edward pointed out that there was no footpath nearby but before any other words could be exchanged, Edward's father was calling out for him, from the direction of Swanwick Lane. Edward headed off over the field to see what the problem was. He found his father and Mr Fielder standing over the body of Dorcas Houghton and was told to run off and get some help.

Police Constable H W Smith was on plain-clothes duty in Osborne Road, Fareham when, at 8.15pm, a young man approached the nearby police station. Constable Smith watched with interest as the young man hesitated for a few minutes and then drew a revolver out of his pocket. Smith did not hesitate. He marched across to the man, and bravely took the gun from him.

'You had better keep me here,' said the man. By this time, Constable Smith had heard about the shooting in Sarisbury so asked the man if his name was Maidment. The man gave the one word reply: 'Yes.' He was then arrested and taken in to the station where, after being searched and interviewed he was charged with wilful murder.

There could be no doubt that Maidment was responsible for the death of Dorcas Houghton. The couple had been seen together just before the shot was fired, Maidment had been seen fleeing the scene, he had the murder weapon with him when he was arrested by Constable Smith and, after being interviewed, had made a full statement admitting that he had shot her. The only defence open to him at his trial would therefore be one of insanity.

That trial opened on 27 June 1899, before Mr Justice Wright. The prosecution was led by Mr C T Giles, assisted by Mr Hunt whilst Maidment's defence rested in the hands of Mr Clavell Salter.

The post-mortem on Dorcas, had been carried out by Dr Cade. He reported a single wound, behind the right ear. He was

also able to tell the court that he had previously attended to
the accused, Maidment, in November 1898. It appeared that
Maidment had purchased the revolver some time before and
on 19 November, he had accidentally shot himself, injuring a
finger on his right hand. Dr Cade had treated Maidment until
17 December and during his various visits had found him silent
and morose.

John Tucker, a fruit-grower, told the court that he was the
prisoner's uncle. Maidment had lived with him for the past two
years. After giving details of the wound, which Maidment had
accidentally inflicted upon himself in November, he turned to
the day of Dorcas' death.

On that morning he had last seen his nephew at around
5.40am. He had been very quiet and somewhat strange the
previous evening and it was clear that he had something on his
mind. In his opinion, Maidment had always been 'not quite
there' and he had often described him as being 'ruled by
the moon', a reference to the idea of mental instability being
governed by the cycles of the moon.

More evidence as to Maidment's possible mental condition
was given by Thomas Cuff, his grandfather. He reported that
his wife's first cousin was in the Dorset County asylum after
attacking his wife with a knife. Another cousin, Samuel Hopkins,
had died in the Fisherton asylum. His own son, also Samuel,
was in the Charminster asylum and his daughter, Harriett, had
suffered from fits all her life. In short, there was the taint of
insanity in his family spanning no less than three generations.

Thomas went on to say that Maidment had lived with him
until two years ago when he had moved in with John Tucker.
His behaviour was always strange. He would scream at night,
say he was going fishing and try to climb out of the window.
On other occasions he would simply sit in a corner crying and
sweating profusely.

Much of this testimony was confirmed by Dr Brown who
had been a medical officer in an asylum and had a great deal
of experience in treating the mentally ill. Prior to the trial, on
18 June, Dr Brown had examined Maidment in prison. He
declared that the prisoner did not have a normal or healthy
mind and showed certain homicidal tendencies.

Unfortunately, the prosecution called Dr T P Richards, the medical officer at Winchester prison. He confirmed that Maidment was admitted to the jail on 20 April and he had kept him under observation ever since. In Dr Richards' opinion, Maidment was certainly depressed but that was common in any prisoner facing such a serious charge. There was no sign or symptom of insanity.

Despite all the evidence as to Maidment's mental problems, the jury still took just ten minutes to decide that he was guilty as charged. Maidment was then sentenced to death and the date for his execution was set.

There may well have been some Home Office disquiet over the possibility that the condemned man was suffering from mental impairment for two medical gentlemen, Dr Brayne and Dr Nicholson, were then sent to Winchester to examine Maidment. They visited him over two days, 6–7 July and submitted their report to the Home Office on 8 July. The basic conclusion of that report was that Maidment was of low intellect and had a somewhat boyish appearance but he was not of unsound mind.

The telegram sent to the Home Office, stating that the execution of Charles Maidment had been carried out satisfactorily.

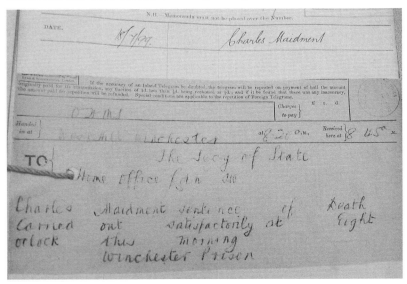

That report, sealed the fate of Charles Maidment. Less than two weeks later, on Tuesday 18 July 1899, he was hanged at Winchester by James Billington as a large crowd gathered outside the prison.

Chapter 5

The Demon Drink
Augustus John Penny
1913

In the year 1898, Augustus John Penny joined the Royal Navy as a stoker. He would serve his country in this way until 1911, forming part of the crew of ships such as the *Victory II*, the *Barham*, the *Duke of Wellington* and the *Drake*. In all that time, Penny was only ever in trouble on a couple of occasions and always for relatively minor offences.

The same could not be said for Penny's mother. Mary Matilda Light had married George Penny when she was twenty-two and very soon afterwards she became addicted to drink. Between 1895 and 1901, she had no less than eight convictions recorded against her, all at Lyndhurst. Of these eight offences, five were for drunkenness, one for using obscene language, and one for common assault. The remaining conviction was for cruelty to her son, Augustus.

It had come to the notice of the authorities that Mary Penny had assaulted her son on 15 November 1896. Both parents were summonsed to appear in court to answer that charge, even though the father, George, had moved out of the house in 1893. In the course of the investigation, officers visited their home at Pollard's Moor, Copythorne. They found the children badly nourished, the floors awash with grease and the house in a generally filthy condition. The stench, it was said, was unbearable and the investigators had to leave the house in order to gulp down some fresh air. In the event, after the evidence had been heard, George Penny was found not guilty but Matilda was convicted and fined. She was also ordered to clean the house up as a matter of urgency. It was hardly surprising then, that Augustus Penny should seek a life away from his mother,

her mistreatment of him, her love of drink and the filthy home he had known.

When Augustus Penny left the Navy, however, he had little choice but to return to his mother's house in Copythorne. From 1911 onwards, there were thus three people living in a somewhat cleaner cottage: Augustus, his mother Matilda and his brother, George Henry. The three operated the farm and the two brothers worked as labourers for their mother.

Matilda, however, had little real interest in the farm and preferred to spend her time drinking. It was perhaps to raise extra cash to fund that habit that, in January 1913, Matilda drew up a document letting all of her land to George, in return for the sum of £12 a year. There was no mention of her other son and naturally this angered Augustus. He made no secret of his disappointment and anger but there was nothing to be done. The deal had been signed but it did nothing to make for a happy household.

On the morning of Sunday, 22 June 1913, George Henry Penny rose from his bed just before 6.00am. At that time his brother was not in the house but he returned soon afterwards and they sat down to eat breakfast together at 8.00am. Three hours later, at 11.00am, George left the house and did not return until 6.00pm. At that time, Matilda asked him to give her sixpence so she could buy some stout. George gave her the money and, soon afterwards, left the house again. He did not return for the night until 11.00pm, by which time it was quite dark.

Without lighting either a lamp or a candle, George made his way to his bed. In order to reach his bedroom he needed to pass through the one occupied by his mother. He crept through very quietly so as not to wake her and as he walked through, he could see the shape of her body in her bed. George's room was now to the left whilst his brother's was to the right. The door to Augustus' room was open and George could see him lying on his bed repeating over and over just two words: 'Oh dear!' George thought nothing of it and retired for the night.

On Monday, 23 June, George rose somewhat earlier, at 5.30am. Once again, Augustus seemed to be already out of the house and, as he passed through his mother's bedroom, George

The church in the village of Copythorne at the time Augustus Penny shot his mother to death.

discovered why this might be. His mother lay dead in her bed, an empty quart bottle on the floor nearby. This was not, however, a case of too much drink, for Matilda had been shot and her blood and brains were spread along the walls and ceiling. George ran off to get help.

By 6.00am, Constable Sydney Joyce was at the cottage. He noted that Matilda lay on her right side with her head resting close to her arm. Seeing that nothing was disturbed, Joyce sent for Superintendent Wakefield and the doctor and then went in search of Augustus Penny.

Some 430 yards away from the cottage, Constable Joyce found Augustus sitting down under a hedge. He was dripping wet and trembling with cold and fear. Joyce escorted his prisoner back to the scene of the shooting and watched as he changed into fresh clothing. Soon after this, Superintendent Wakefield arrived, took charge of Augustus and escorted him to the police station in a motor car.

Augustus readily admitted his guilt and made a full written statement outlining what had taken place at the cottage. That statement read: 'On Sunday, about seven o'clock I took a quart bottle and went to the Compass. I had two pints of beer and took a quart bottle home to my mother. About eight-thirty I went upstairs. She was asleep. I woke her and we drank the quart of beer between us. I left the bottle by the side of the bed. She laid down and I went to my bedroom and got the gun and as I came through my mother's bedroom she was lying on the bed. I held the gun up with the point towards my mother's head and it went off.'

'I had no idea the gun was loaded when the gun went off. I could see what I had done which frightened me. I ran out of the house with the gun and jumped in the stream and left the gun there.'

The suggestion was that whilst it had been extremely fool-hardy to point a gun at someone, the actual shooting had been a terrible accident. Nevertheless, Augustus was charged with murder and began to make appearances before the magistrates and the coroner's court.

It was after a brief appearance at the magistrates' court that Augustus said that he wished to make another statement. He was, quite properly, cautioned and his new statement was then written down. In this second document, Augustus began: 'Last Sunday I got up about four o'clock, took the gun I had borrowed from Cull on the Saturday night and went into our meadows to try to shoot pigeons. I could not get any but shot and wounded one, but did not find it.'

'I returned home about seven o'clock and got the breakfast. My brother George returned about eight o'clock. I poured the tea and took some upstairs to my mother. Then me and George sat down and had breakfast together. George and me got the cabbage and potatoes ready and I put them in the pot.'

'George left home about eleven o'clock. I then again went into the field as my mother was then downstairs, to look for the wounded pigeon, but could not find it. I returned home and Herbert Hunt came for George to shave him, but George was out and I shaved him.'

'Me and my mother had dinner together and about two o'clock I went to the Coach at Cadmann and had two pints of beer. I left the Coach at two-thirty and returned home.'

'About five o'clock, me and my mother had tea. About six o'clock George came in and had his tea. Mother asked him for some money to get some stout. He gave her sixpence. I said:

"I have a bottle of stout in the cupboard." I got it and gave it to her.'

'My brother left about quarter past six and I went to the *Compass*, had two pints of beer and took my mother back a quart of fives [a type of beer] in the bottle. I got back home about half past eight. Mother was in bed upstairs. I went up and asked her if she would take a drink. She said yes and we had the quart of beer between us.'

'I then asked my mother if she was warm enough and she said: "Yes, but you can put the old coat on my feet" which I did. She then began abusing me and said: "If it was not for George I would not have a bite or a drop." She also said that she would sell the hay when it was up and she and George would go away and I could go to the devil. I said: "For God's sake, lie down and go to sleep" but she would not.'

'She would not shut up and I lost my temper with her as she tormented me about George. I lost all control of myself, went to my bedroom, got the gun and before I could cool my temper I shot her in the head. She exasperated me so much. I lost all control of myself but I did not mean to kill her and I am very sorry for it now and I must put up with it.'

Augustus Penny finally appeared before Mister Justice Low, to face the charge of murder on Saturday, 8 November 1913. His defence rested in the hands of Mr Blake Ogden whilst the case for the Crown was led by Mr G W Ricketts, who was assisted by Mr E Duke. Amongst the early witnesses were those who could confirm Augustus Penny's movements on the day of the shooting.

Bertie James Cull was the man who actually owned the gun used to shoot Matilda. He reported that on Saturday, 21 June, he had been drinking in the *Horse and Groom* at around 9.30pm. Augustus was also in the bar and asked Bertie if he might borrow his gun so that he could shoot some pigeons. Bertie said that he could have it the following morning but Augustus said that he'd rather have it that same night if it wasn't too much trouble. As a result, they walked back to Bertie's farm where the gun was kept in a cowshed. Bertie handed the weapon over but first checked that it wasn't loaded. Finally, Bertie confirmed that he did not give Augustus any cartridges.

Stephen Dowding was the licensee of the *Compass Inn* and he testified that Augustus had come into his pub on the evening of Sunday, 22 June 22. He was sober when he left at 8.45pm. The Penny cottage was some one and a half miles from the *Compass*. This was confirmed by Emily Dowding, Stephen's wife. She was also able to add that when Augustus left, he took with him a quart of beer in a bottle.

On the way back to his cottage, Augustus had been met by William Barnes, a bricklayer. It was then around 9.00pm on the Sunday and Augustus was some eighty yards from his home. He appeared to be in a happy mood and bade Barnes a cheery 'Goodnight.' Barnes too confirmed that Augustus appeared to be sober.

Not long after this meeting, Herbert William Hunt walked past the Penny cottage on the way to his own home which was the next house along the lane. He reported that as he passed he heard loud talking coming from inside the Penny home but he would not say that it was an argument.

Police sergeant Ernest Thomas Long had taken charge of the shotgun once it had been recovered from a stream, close to where Augustus had been found underneath the hedge. The normal pull of such a weapon would be from five to seven pounds but he had tested the gun used to kill Matilda and found that it required a pull of thirteen pounds. Sergeant Long had also searched the cottage and reported that he had found a bag containing six cartridges, in the kitchen. They were a mixed bunch of cartridges but two were similar to the spent one found in the gun.

Medical evidence was given by the police surgeon, Dr Barrington White. He had first examined Matilda's body in situ and found her head much damaged by the shotgun blast. Blood and brains were scattered on three sides of the room and the ceiling and part of Matilda's cranial bone lay on the floor near the bed. He had made his initial examination at 9.10am on Monday 23 June and estimated time of death at between ten and twelve hours earlier.

Dr White was also able to say that the gun must have been fired from close range and by someone in a standing position, aiming the weapon downwards. The suggestion was that Matilda in tomorrow, may throw fresh light upon the relations between prisoner and his mother.

18.11.13.

I have consulted the Commissioner who does not think that the evidence of provocation was sufficiently strong to justify a recommendation to mercy. No interference. R.M.K.

18.11.13.

Confirmation from the Home Secretary's Office that no grounds could be found for commuting Penny's death sentence.

The reply to the Home Office, confirming that Penny had now been told that the death sentence would be carried out.

Sir,   24th November, *1913*.

Re A. J. Penny. 244,823.

On behalf of the High Sheriff for the County of Hants, I have the honour to acknowledge due receipt of your letter of 22nd inst stating that the Secretary of State has failed to discover any sufficient ground to justify him in advising His Majesty to interfere with the due course of law. The convict has been informed of this and the sentence of death passed on him at the recent Assizes will be duly carried into effect on Wednesday morning next 26th inst at 8 a.m.

I am,
Sir,
Your obedient Servant,

was lying down, with her back to the door which led to the other bedrooms and the gun had been fired at her from near that doorway. Matilda's hair was singed and the gun would have been between one and a half and two and a half feet from her head when it was fired.

After every death sentence is carried out, an inquest must be held. This is the standard report on an executed prisoner, showing that the sentence had been carried out on Augustus John Penny.

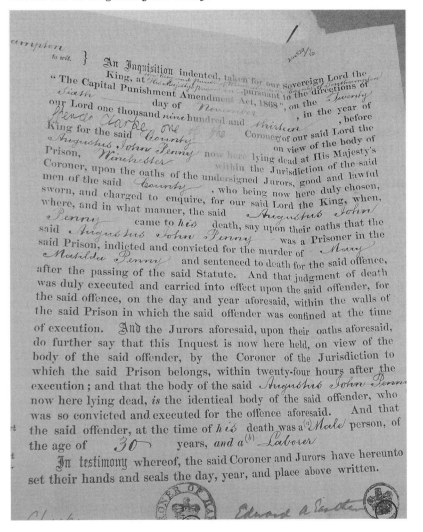

The verdict was, in reality, a foregone conclusion. There could be no denying that Augustus had shot his mother dead and was therefore guilty of murder but the jury still took twenty-five minutes to return their verdict. When the verdict did come, the jury added a recommendation to mercy on account of the treatment Augustus had received from his mother during his life.

It did nothing to save the life of Augustus Penny and less than three weeks later, on Wednesday, 26 November 1913, he was hanged at Winchester by John Ellis and Albert Lumb. As for the shotgun used to kill Matilda Penny, local legend has it that it later passed into the hands of a farmer, Mr Evelyn Light, who used it for years afterwards – to shoot rabbits!

Chapter 6

The Southampton Garage Murder
William Henry Podmore
1930

Vivian Messiter had led a most interesting life. Born on 1 September 1871 in Wincanton, he had been educated at Trent College, near Nottingham. His ambition was to enter the field of medicine and for that reason he enrolled at Edinburgh University in 1889. He hadn't been there very long, however, before he realised that becoming a doctor wasn't for him after all. He dropped out and began to travel.

Messiter's first port of call was Mexico. From there he travelled to Denver where, in 1897, he married Sarah Eleanor Culley. She gave birth to a daughter in 1899 but Vivian and Sarah separated in 1905 and he moved on to New York. Tragically, the daughter would be killed in a car crash in the early 1920s.

In the early part of the twentieth century, Messiter could see the dark clouds of war looming over Europe and decided that he wished to serve the country of his birth. He returned to England before 1914 and, on 30 August 1915, enlisted in the 17th Service Battalion of the Northumberland Fusiliers as a 2nd Lieutenant. On 18 May 1916, Messiter was promoted to Lieutenant and, almost exactly a year later, on 1 May 1917, reached the rank of Captain. That was the rank he still held at the end of the war when Messiter was discharged for medical reasons. He had been wounded and would, for the rest of his life, walk with a limp.

Once hostilities were at an end, Messiter joined Vickers at Enfield as an engineer, but soon he returned to New York where he met Mrs Mary Nevin. They came back to England together in July 1928 and lived as man and wife at 51 Ebury Street, London. The relationship didn't last and even though they remained on good terms, Mrs Nevin returned to New York soon afterwards. Messiter was now at a loose end. He needed some new position to occupy his mind. It was with some excitement that, on 10 September 1928, he found himself appointed sales manager for the Wolf's Head Oil Company.

The duties were simple enough. Wolf's Head was an American oil company and they wished to break into the British market, starting in the south of England. Messiter was given a float of £100 to finance the set-up of a sales force and was told to draw £10 per week for himself as a salary. A regional office, which was really little more than an old garage to be used as a depot for storage, was rented at 42 Grove Street, Southampton, and Messiter moved to that city at the end of September, taking lodgings with Alva and Gertrude Parrott at 3 Carlton Road.

Messiter threw himself into his work, placing a total of six advertisements in the *Southern Daily Echo*, seeking people who wished to work as agents on commission. He had a number of replies and did take on a few applicants. Everything seemed to be going well. The first delivery of oil to the depot in Grove Street was made, a few orders came in and were duly filled but then, on Tuesday 30 October 1928, Vivian Messiter simply disappeared.

One thing that could be said about Vivian Messiter was that he was a creature of habit. He left his lodgings at the same time every day. He would break for lunch at the same time. He returned home at the same time every evening, and was certainly not the type of man to leave without any explanation. Besides, none of his belongings had been removed from his lodgings. Mr Parrott was growing rather concerned and since he was an ex-policeman, he was not about to let the matter drop.

Alva Sidney Havergill Parrott went to the office at Grove Street but the place was securely locked and there was no sign of life. By 1 November, there had still been no sign of Messiter so Mr Parrott telephoned the police station at Bargate and reported him as a missing person. The local police showed little

A page of the expenses book kept by Vivian Messiter and in his own hand. Notice that four gallons of 'gas' or petrol, cost just 5s 3d – approximately 26p!

interest in the matter and made no real efforts to discover what might have happened. After all, Messiter had a history of travel and it was assumed that he had simply moved on yet again.

Two days later, on 3 November, Mr Parrott wrote to the head office of the Wolf's Head Company at 107 Old Broad Street, London and reported Messiter's disappearance to them. Further, he went on to say that since he had to be in London on business on 5 November, he would like to meet an officer of the company and discuss the matter further.

That meeting did indeed take place, at Waterloo station, and Mr Parrott repeated his concerns. The company also seemed to take little interest, not even being too concerned that this might be costing them business. In fact, the only sign of interest displayed by the company was to send a letter to Mr Parrott, which he received on 7 November, asking for any communications he might receive for Mr Messiter be forwarded on to them in London.

Not one to be dissuaded, on 8 November, Mr Parrott took his concerns to the St Mary's police station in Southampton, where he spoke to Chief Inspector Parker and asked if he would send an officer to the depot. Parker agreed and later that day, at around 8.00pm, Mr Parrott, Sergeant Hayward and a uniformed constable went to Grove Street. A cursory examination of the premises was made and at one stage, a glance through one of the windows revealed that the car Messiter had been supplied with, a maroon Morris Oxford, registration BW 9101, was parked inside the garage.

On 9 November, Mr Parrott wrote to the Wolf's Head Company again to say that the car they had given Messiter was secure inside the garage. This, finally, spurred them into some sort of action. Mr Greenall, one of the directors, visited New Scotland Yard and added his concerns to those of Mr Parrott. He was told to talk to the police in Southampton but at least photographs of the missing man, together with a full description, appeared in the *Police Gazette* on 5 December.

The New Year dawned and the Wolf's Head company finally decided that someone else had to take over from Messiter. On 8 January 1929, they appointed a new sales manager, Henry Obadiah Stanley Passmore, who lived at Northlands Road, Southampton. Two days later, on Thursday, 10 January, Mr Passmore and Mr Bailey, a junior clerk from Jenkins and Sons, a firm of solicitors, visited the depot at 42 Grove Street.

The two men forced the lock and, finally, Passmore gained entrance to the garage. The first thing that Passmore examined was the car itself. Inside he found a torch and a pair of gloves and on the back seat, some drums of oil with an overcoat thrown over them. Looking further around the garage, Passmore saw that there were boxes stacked about the place, containing cans of oil. Some of these stacks formed a sort of corridor along the back wall and it was there that Henry Passmore found a body, which appeared to bear a gun-shot wound to the head. The mystery of the disappearance of Vivian Messiter had been solved.

The first police officer on the scene was Constable Horace Robert George Hellyer. He arrived at 11.15am, to be followed, ten minutes later by Chief Inspector William Henry Parker. The two policemen made a careful inspection of the premises. Messiter's body lay on its back, his left arm lying across his chest, his right arm bent vertically from the elbow. He was fully dressed in a brown overall and wore kid gloves on both hands. His legs were apart, with his feet pointing outwards.

Messiter's head was in an advanced state of decomposition and it appeared that rats had attacked his eyes, the left side of his face, his mouth, the right side of his chin, both ears and his nose. There was a gaping wound around one eye socket. This looked like a shooting, but it would be for a post-mortem to determine the exact cause of death.

It was clear that the local force would require some assistance in the investigation so later that same day, at 6.45pm, a telegram was despatched to Scotland Yard, by Mr McCormac, the Chief Constable of Southampton, asking for assistance. The following day, Detective Chief Inspector Prothero and Detective Sergeant Young arrived in Southampton, from London.

The post-mortem on the dead man was conducted by Dr George Robert Seager Thomas, on the same day that the body was found: 10 January 1929. He noted that the parts of the body that had been covered, were quite well preserved but those exposed to the elements had deteriorated substantially. Dr Thomas was, however, able to refute the initial belief that Vivian Messiter had been shot. He reported that one or more blows from a heavy, blunt instrument, had been the cause of death.

Up to this point, the efforts of the Southampton police had not been of the highest quality. They had taken little real interest in the original disappearance of Mr Messiter and had

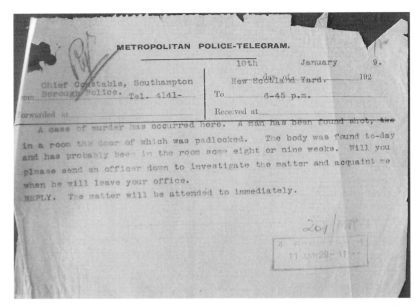

The telegram sent from the Southampton police to Scotland Yard, asking for assistance.

only made somewhat cursory examinations of the premises before the body was discovered. Now, this level of inefficiency seemed to continue. It was not until 12 January that Acting Sergeant Turner found a small gold swivel from a watch. It seemed that the killer, whoever he was, had torn Messiter's watch from his person, causing the swivel to fracture and come away.

More serious, perhaps, was the fact that it was not until 13 January that Detective Constable William Barber found a hammer lying between two oil drums close to the wall. The head of the hammer was resting on the ground with the handle pointing upwards. The head and shaft of the hammer bore bloodstains and there were what appeared to be hairs adhering to it; one on the head and one on the wood of the handle. This hammer would eventually be shown to be the murder weapon.

On that same day, 13 January, Acting Sergeant Turner found a piece of paper lying in some sawdust on the floor. The paper was a memorandum relating to a shipment of 36 gallons of oil but of more significance was what was written on the back. This was a receipt for ten shillings rent, signed by someone named John Robert Horne and showed that it had been received from someone named Mr Thomas.

Further evidence relating to this Mr Thomas was discovered the following day, 14 January, again by Acting Sergeant Turner. This item was a screwed up piece of paper, found in a store-room. When unfolded it was seen that this was a short letter which read: 'Mr W.F. Thomas. I shall be at 42 Grove St at 10am but not noon.' and was signed 'V. Messiter'.

The two officers from Scotland Yard had, by now, also discovered other items of interest. An order book had been found in the garage but some pages appeared to have been torn out. In addition, carbon sheets in the back of that same book, bore impressions of various orders for oil which appeared to be fictitious. One, for example, related to an order from a company named Cromer and Barrett of 25 Bold Street, Southampton. There was no such company trading anywhere within the Southampton area and Bold Street itself, did not exist.

A search of Messiter's lodgings had also revealed various letters replying to his advertisements for agents to sell the oil. One of these was from a W F Thomas and gave the address of

The note, found crumpled at the murder scene, which gave police officer's investigating Messiter's murder, the name W F Thomas.

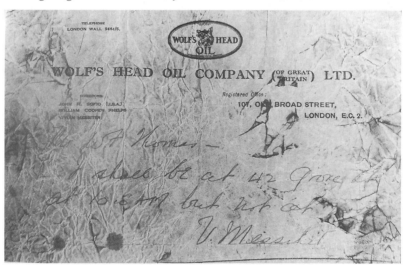

A legitimate receipt found in one of Messiter's record books at the storeroom. Note the indentations on the page, from the one above, which had been torn out of the book.

5 Cranberry Avenue. However, when officers checked out that address, they discovered that Mr Thomas had left Southampton on 3 November 1928.

This was a most curious discovery. It was now believed that Vivian Messiter had, in all probability, been killed on the same day that he was last seen at his lodgings: Tuesday, 30 October 1928. Mr Thomas, must have been one of his agents since a receipt belonging to him had been found at the garage and this same Thomas had left Southampton on Saturday, 3 November, just five days later. A description of Thomas was taken and circulated widely to police stations, along with that of a blonde-haired woman who had lived with him and was described as his wife.

On 15 January 1929, Sir Bernard Spilsbury, the Home Office pathologist, travelled down to Southampton and, with Dr George Thomas, performed a second post-mortem on Messiter. His subsequent report stated that three separate blows had been rained down upon Messiter's head and it was most likely that the first had been struck from behind whilst Messiter was bending down. Two further blows from the hammer had then been given resulting in massive fractures of the skull. One of the

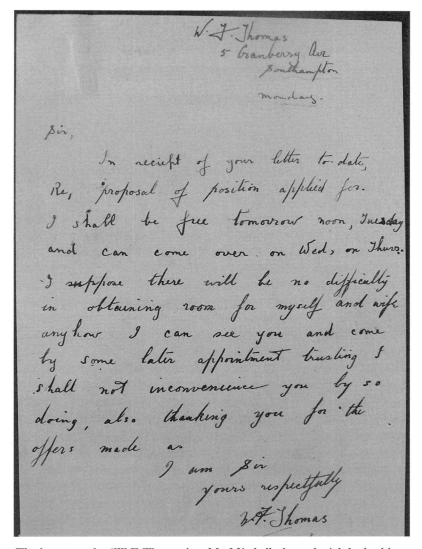

The letter sent by 'W F Thomas' to Mr Mitchell about the job he had been offered. Note that the letter carries the correct Southampton address used by Podmore.

blows had landed in the region of the left eyebrow, causing a gaping hole, which subsequently had been widened by the action of rats. It was this wound which had originally looked as if it might have been caused by a bullet.

The description of W F Thomas brought information from two other police forces. Officers at Salisbury stated that a man fitting that description, and using the name Thomas, had been suspected of stealing some wage packets from his employer at Downton, near Salisbury. In addition, Manchester police reported that this man was also wanted for the theft of a car in their area. There, however, he had been using the name Podmore and travelling with one Lily Hambleton whose home address was 32 Buxton Street, Hanley. A search of police records showed that William Henry Podmore had a long criminal record with a number of convictions in three different names; Podmore, Stubbs and Nicholls. The police now knew precisely who they were looking for.

The description of Podmore was now given out to the gentlemen of the press. It read: 'Police are anxious to trace the whereabouts of a man giving the name of William Frank Thomas. Age about 32, height 5 feet 4 or 5 inches, complexion pale, hair dark, clean shaven, has a distinctive scar about one inch in length on his temple.'

'Lived at 5 Cranberry Ave, Southampton, from about the 20th October to 3rd November, 1928, with a woman age about 30, height about 5 feet 3 inches, complexion pale, hair golden, believed to be dyed.'

'These persons went to reside at Downton, Wiltshire on or about 3 November 1928, leaving there on 22 December during which time Thomas was employed at Mitchells Saw Mills, Lode Hill, Downton.'

Since one part of Podmore's description related to a small scar he had over one eyebrow, this factor was a hook, which the press latched on to and all the reports referred to the search for the 'man with the scar'. As for his girlfriend, since she had blonde hair, she was referred to as 'Golden-haired Lil'.

On 17 January, officers in Southampton received a telephone call from their colleagues in Staffordshire. Lily Hambleton had apparently returned to her home address in Hanley. She was immediately interviewed and explained that until recently, she and Podmore had been in Birmingham. They had seen newspaper reports of the Southampton murder and talked about what they should do next. Podmore said that she should return home and he would go back to Southampton in order to clear his name. As Lily had travelled to Hanley, Podmore had gone down to London with the intention of going on to Southampton the following day. Finally, Lily was able to say that Podmore would be staying overnight at the *Leicester Hotel* on Vauxhall Bridge Road, a place they had stayed before and where they used to work.

On the morning of 18 January 1929, Detective Inspector Charles Simmonds went to the *Leicester Hotel* and arrested Podmore. It should be noted that Podmore had signed in at the Leicester, using his real name. Podmore was then escorted to the Gerald Road police station for interview.

The police believed that they had captured the man responsible for the murder of Vivian Messiter but they had no real evidence to back up a charge. No fingerprints of any kind had been found on the hammer. The officers did, however, have one thing

Details of William Podmore's criminal convictions, as detailed by the police.

Sentence	Court.	Date.	Offence.	Name in which convicted.
Probation 12 mths sent to) Akbar Refty.)	Stoke-on-T.	6/7/11.	Housebkg.	Wm.Hy. Podmore
	" "	21/6/15.	Stealing cash box £2.9.0.	Ditto.
3 years B.I. & 1 day concur.	Knutsford Sess.Altrincham	4/7/17.	Housebkg.	Ditto
B.0.12 mos £5.	Leek Sess Staffs	6/1/20.	Stealing motor cycle.	Ditto.
42/- or 1 mth	Warrington Boro'	18/8/25.	Stealing bicycles 2 cases.	Frank Stubbs.
42/- or 1 mth conct.	" "	"		
4, 4, & 4 mos H.L.	"	"	28/11/25	Stealing motor covers (3 cases).	Frank Nicholls.
10,10, & 10 mos concur.	Leicester City Qtr. Sessions	4/4/27.	Stg cheque book false pretences & attd. false pretences.	Wm. Hy.Podmore.

CONVICTIONS AGAINST WILLIAM HENRY PODMORE, C. R. O. No.18029/18.

on their side. Podmore, alias Thomas, was wanted for two other offences and could be charged with them, tried for them and, if found guilty, be sentenced for them.

Initially, Podmore was charged with the theft of a motor vehicle at Manchester. He was tried in that city on 29 January 1929 and sentenced to six months' imprisonment. He originally began to serve that sentence at Strangeways prison but was transferred to Winchester so that he could attend the inquest on Messiter, as a witness. Not surprisingly, the inquest eventually returned a verdict of murder by person or persons unknown and Podmore was returned to Winchester prison to finish off his sentence.

On 29 June, Podmore was released from prison but immediately re-arrested at the gates and charged with the second offence of theft. This related to the stealing of wage packets at Downton.

After Podmore and Lily Hambleton had left Southampton on 3 November, he had started work as a mechanic for a building contractor at Downton. On Saturday, 22 December 1928, a number of wage packets had gone missing. Podmore, who at the time, was still using the name Thomas, was questioned by Superintendent Charles Townsend of the Salisbury police. He was asked where precisely he had worked prior to coming to Downton and said that he had been a tyre-fitter for the Allied Transport Company in Bold Street, Southampton. He also stated, correctly, that he had lodged at 5 Cranberry Avenue.

There were other people to interview and Thomas was allowed to go after he had been questioned. The following day, 23 December, he and Lily vanished and, of course, the company he told them he had worked for and the address he gave for their offices, both proved to be fictitious.

On 15 July 1929, Podmore was transferred to Wandsworth prison. Two days later, on 17 July, he was tried at the Central Criminal Court, found guilty of the Downton theft and sentenced to a further six months in prison. He would be due for release on 17 December.

This sentence raises an interesting point, which we will return to later but the police had all the evidence they would ever gather on the Messiter murder, in their hands, by the end of May or beginning of June, 1929. Despite this, Podmore was not charged with the murder at this time. Instead, the police preferred to have him sentenced to another six months in prison, for theft. It was what would happen inside that prison that would cause a number of people to come to eventually believe that a possible miscarriage of justice might have taken place.

William Henry Podmore was duly released from prison on 17 December and once again, was re-arrested at the gates. This time he was indeed charged with the murder of Vivian Messiter. After various appearances before the magistrates, he finally faced his trial at Winchester, before the Lord Chief Justice, Lord Hewart, on 3 March 1930. The trial would last until 8 March, during which Podmore was defended by Mr H du Parcq and Mr T R C Goff. The case for the Crown was led by Sir Thomas Inskip, who was assisted by Mr J G Trapnell.

Harold Frederick Galton was another of the men who, on 28 October 1928, had replied to the advertisement placed by Messiter. Galton had managed to sell a five gallon shipment of oil to Stanley Grover of Nursling Farm and, on the evening of 29 October, Messiter had written out a receipt and got Galton to sign it. This transaction was perfectly legitimate but the page prior to this, in Messiter's book, had been torn out.

It was soon noticed that Galton's signed receipt bore indentations from that now missing page. It was not until 7 March 1929, whilst Podmore was in prison, that this receipt was examined more carefully. A powerful light was shone, at an angle, onto the receipt and this revealed the writing from the page above. This had been photographed and was now introduced into evidence. The previous page had been a receipt, dated 28 October 1928 and read:

Received from Wolf's Head Oil Company, commission on Cromer and Barrett, 5 galls at 6d, 2/6d.

It was signed, WFT – W F Thomas, the name Podmore had been using. The company named, did not exist. The inference was clear; Podmore had been submitting false orders and claiming commissions he was not entitled to. This was held to be the motive for Messiter's murder. He had discovered the subterfuge and had no doubt threatened Podmore with the police and had been killed in order to prevent this.

Although Podmore denied it throughout his trial, there is a good deal of evidence that he was indeed stealing from Messiter. A number of receipts were produced in court giving names and address such as; Bold Street, Southampton; Baskerfield of Clayton Farm near Winchester and Ben Jervis of The Crescent, Bassett. All of these were shown to be fictitious, but an examination of Podmore's past showed that he had links with people and places of a similar name. Thus, he had known a Bold Street in Warrington, a man named Baskeyfield, which was similar to one of the names, and another named Jarvis, again a close approximation. It was too much for coincidence and pointed to a systematic fraud, but did it point to murder? It was true that Podmore had a string of previous convictions for fraud and theft but none had ever involved any degree of violence.

Another witness, Henry Marsh, also did little for the prosecution's case. Henry lived at 8 Oakfield Mansions, Grosvenor Square, Southampton and was an engineer at the Morris Motor works. Some time in October 1928 he lent his somewhat distinctive hammer to a man and never had it returned to him. Once the body of Messiter had been discovered, pictures and a description of the murder weapon were published and Marsh came forward to positively identify it as his property. He had subsequently attended an identification parade where he failed to pick out Podmore as the man he had given the hammer to. Another man from the Morris Motor Works, who had seen the exchange of the hammer, also failed to pick out Podmore as the man it had been loaned to.

A watch had been taken from Messiter's body and this had been found, by a plumber, hidden in the cistern of a public convenience, situated at the junction of West Marlands Road and Windsor Road, in Southampton. The watch was only found some four weeks before Podmore's trial for murder began. It bore a distinctive crest, and the initials VM, which was possibly why no attempt had been made to sell it to a dealer. It had certainly belonged to Messiter for some keys were found with it. Two of these fitted a trunk that had belonged to Messiter and been left behind in his lodgings. Attempts were made to show that Podmore had knowledge of this particular convenience but he denied knowing anything about it.

On 20 October 1928, the day that Messiter was probably murdered, Podmore had travelled to Salisbury with Lily Hambleton in regard to the position at Downton. Lily testified that they had driven up in a red Morris Oxford, which, allowing for the discrepancy of colour, was probably Messiter's car. Indeed, Podmore freely admitted that he had driven Messiter's car to Salisbury.

Continuing her evidence, Lily stated that on that day, Podmore had left their lodgings at some time between 10.00am and 10.30am. She next saw him at 1.00pm when he came home for lunch. He told her he had been working on Messiter's car but had now finished and was going to drive it over to Salisbury to deliver some oil. He then returned to Grove Street to pick the vehicle up.

At 2.00pm, Lily met Podmore, with the car, at the top of Cranberry Street. They drove towards Salisbury, finally returning to Southampton for around 5.30pm when Podmore said he had to return the car. He got back to their lodgings at about 5.50pm.

The inference from the prosecution was that Podmore had killed Messiter and then used his car to attend a meeting with his next employer at Downton. Business concluded he had then driven the car back to Grove Street and abandoned it, locking it in the storeroom along with the dead body of Vivian Messiter.

The next two witnesses were ones whose testimony, when examined, should have been rated as totally worthless. They were two convicts who had been in prison with Podmore at Wandsworth and the stories they told were full of contradictions.

The first of these was David Cummings, a Scot, who had gone into Wandsworth on 27 June 1929. It was widely known, throughout the prison, that Podmore was the man suspected of the Southampton murder and, according to Cummings, the two fell into conversation a number of times, especially on exercise. They spoke about the murder and discussed the evidence against Podmore.

According to Cummings, at one stage they spoke about the murder weapon and Cummings had said: 'It was rather funny that they found your fingerprints on the hammer.' To this, Podmore was said to have replied: 'It is quite natural Jock. The hammer belonged to me. I was working with the hammer.'

This is an absolutely astounding statement. Chief Inspector Harry Battley was the head of the fingerprint department at Scotland Yard and he had made a careful examination of the hammer. No prints whatsoever were detected and yet, according to Cummins, Podmore was admitting that there was a legitimate reason for his prints to be on the murder weapon by claiming ownership of it. Further, the court had already heard that the weapon had actually belonged to Henry Marsh and no link with Podmore had been shown.

On another occasion, Cummings claimed that Podmore had actually confessed to the murder saying: 'I went to steal the car but I had no intention of killing the man.' Yet it was on record that soon after his admission into Wandsworth, Podmore had asked to be separated from the other men as they were talking to him about the murder and asking him questions. This is the same man who then, apparently, made a full confession to one of the other inmates!

Even more contentious was the testimony of the second convict, Joseph Deass, a negro, who was actually still in Wandsworth and was brought to court under guard to testify against Podmore. Deass said that one day, on exercise, Podmore had said that he wanted to tell him everything. He then continued to tell a story which contained, amongst other elements, the 'fact' that Podmore had; '...worked eleven months with that man in the garage.' One day, Podmore had asked Messiter for some money but he had refused. They had argued and Messiter had used bad language to Podmore whereupon he had picked up the hammer and hit him. He had then left Southanpton that same afternoon.

There are two major mistakes with this so-called testimony. First, Podmore had only worked for Messiter for two days, not the eleven months Deass claimed. Secondly, Podmore had not left Southampton until 3 November, five days after Messiter was killed. In short, both of these witnesses were seemingly being rather economical with the truth, yet this was the only extra 'evidence' the police had collected after June 1929.

Of more importance perhaps was the testimony of William John Streets. He had been a prisoner at Winchester where he was sent in February 1929 for non-payment of rates. At one stage Podmore asked him if he came from Southampton and when he said that he did, Podmore asked Streets if he knew when the inquest on Messiter was to take place. The two then fell into conversation about the crime and at one stage Podmore said: 'They had about sixteen hours at me down yonder, but I am not the man. I shall be glad when it is all over as I am innocent of the job.'

In fact, the police had a third convict witness at their disposal. William Goulden had also been in Wandsworth and he had testified at Messiter's inquest, saying that he too had had conversations with Podmore in which he had admitted his guilt. So weak was his evidence that he wasn't even called at Podmore's trial.

The time came for Podmore to take the stand and give his own version of events. He stated that on 23 October 1928, he had replied to two advertisements in the local newspaper. The first of these was to Mr Messiter and the second was to Mr Joseph George Stuart Mitchell of Woodfields, Salisbury, about the position at Downton. Both letters were written in the name of William F Thomas.

Mr Mitchell contacted him the next day and made arrangements to meet at Bargate on Saturday, 27 October at 5.00pm. The two men met, as arranged, and later Mitchell wrote to 'Thomas' offering him a month's trial at £2 10s a week. Podmore accepted but unfortunately, Mitchell was not in a position to take him on immediately and, since he had had a favourable reply from Mr Messiter, he started work for him on 28 October. It was always intended to be just a temporary position until he could take up the employment with Mr Mitchell.

Podmore, perhaps rather foolishly, continued to deny that he had been defrauding Messiter, saying that the fictitious addresses referred to in court were on a list given to him by Messiter. He had spent a good few hours searching for these addresses, obviously without luck. It was pure coincidence that some bore a resemblance to names connected to his past.

On 20 October 20, Podmore had been working on Messiter's car and at lunchtime, returned to his landlady's house to say that he would be leaving soon. This, of course, was because he was due to take the position with Mr Mitchell. At the time he was dressed in dungarees and his hands were dirty from his work on the car. These facts were indeed confirmed by his landlady, Mrs Horne.

Podmore admitted that he had used Messiter's car to visit Mr Mitchell that same afternoon, taking Lily Hambleton with him. Messiter had given his permission for the use of the car as it needed a run to test it after Podmore had worked on it. At the meeting with Mitchell, Podmore confirmed that he had finished work in Southampton and was ready to start work for him. Mitchell told him that he wasn't needed until the following Monday, 5 November.

On 3 November, the day they finally left Southampton, Podmore and Lily arrived at Downton at around noon. Podmore said that he had lost his wallet and Mr Mitchell loaned him £1 against his first wage packet. The matter of the later theft of the wage packets had already been dealt with and Podmore admitted that he had left the district in order to avoid arrest. Soon afterwards, he had seen an advertisement for a position at the *Stonebridge Hotel*, Meridien and Podmore had replied. He was interviewed by the proprietor, Alfred Charles Crumbleholme, on 31 December, after which both Podmore and Lily were taken on at a combined wage of £2 per week. They started work there on 4 January 1929.

Much had been made of the fact that Podmore had suddenly left the hotel, without picking up his wages, soon after details of the Southampton murder had appeared in the newspapers. The prosecution claimed that this was a sign of guilt but Podmore said that the hours had been unbearable and he had tried to get his wages but the manager said it would have to wait until after the stocks were checked. Podmore had simply been unwilling to wait.

He and Lily had then travelled to the Potteries, then to Birmingham where he had seen reports of the police wishing

Whitehall,
    London, S.W.1.   31st May, 1929.
and the following number
quoted :-
        148   of   1929.

Your reference: 201/STN/1.

            Sir,

                    re Vivian Messiter deceased.

            Referring to your letter of the 1st February forwarding
    for my information, a Police Report made by Chief Inspector
    Prothero, and copies of the statements of witnesses taken in
    the course of the inquiries which he had made, I have to
    state that I have now had under consideration a further
    Police Report setting out in detail the proceedings of the
    Coroner's Inquest (when a verdict of murder against some
    person or persons unknown was returned), and the result of
    certain inquiries which have been made since the Inquest.
    After consulting Mr Trapnell, the Counsel who attended the
    Inquest on behalf of the Chief Constable of Southampton, I
    have decided, upon a review of the whole of the evidence
    available, that it is not sufficiently strong to render it
    probable that a jury would convict the man Podmore, who has
    come under grave suspicion.

            The case has been investigated with great perseverance
    under considerable handicaps in respect of time and otherwise

                            I am, Sir,
The Commissioner of Police   Your obedient Servant,
    of the Metropolis,
        New Scotland Yard,   (sgd) S. Pearce
            S.W.1.
                            Assistant Director.

*A letter, sent from the office of the Director of Public Prosecutions to
Scotland Yard. Dated 31 May 1929, it clearly states that there is not
sufficient evidence against Podmore on the charge of murder, yet after this
date the only 'new evidence' were the statements of Podmore's fellow
prisoners, which were shown to be filled with inaccuracies.*

to interview him. Podmore had wanted to go to Southampton
and travelled down to London for that purpose. Once in the
Capital, he had tried to telephone Scotland Yard, to tell them
he was on his way to Southampton but there was something
wrong with the line. He added that the fault might have been

with the call-box he was using, rather that with the police line. Asked why he had simply not handed himself in at Scotland Yard which was only a one penny bus ride from the *Leicester Hotel*, Podmore said that he had no intention of handing himself in to the London police. His intention was just to let them know that he would be in Southampton the next day.

Was Podmore's story plausible? That was for the jury to decide and, in the event, they decided that Podmore was guilty as charged. He was then sentenced to death by Lord Hewart. An appeal was immediately entered.

That appeal was heard on 7 April 1930 before Justices Avory, Branson and Finlay. There were two grounds to the appeal; that evidence had been admitted which ought not to have been and that the judges summing up had been misdirection. The evidence, which the defence held should not have been admitted was, of course, the testimony of the two prisoners both of whom said that Podmore had confessed his guilt to them. Without this, the evidence was purely circumstantial and it had to be remembered that Podmore had never been found guilty of any other offence involving violence. Despite the doubts, the appeal court judges ruled that there had been sufficient evidence to convict and the summing up had been perfectly fair. The appeal was dismissed.

On Tuesday, 22 April 1930, William Henry Podmore, possibly an innocent man, was hanged at Winchester by Thomas Pierrepoint and Alfred Allen. Only three other men were hanged in a British prison in that year: Sidney Harry Fox for the murder of his mother at Margate; Samuel Cushnan for the murder of a postman in Northern Ireland and Albert Edward Marjeram for the motiveless stabbing of Edith May Parker at Dartford Heath in Kent.

Chapter 7

The Murder Without a Body
James Camb
1947

On Friday, 10 October 1947, the Union Castle line ship *Durban Castle* left Capetown in South Africa, bound for Southampton. Amongst the passengers was a young actress, Eileen Isabella Ronnie Gibson, known as Gay, who occupied a first-class cabin, number 126 on B deck.

Gay Gibson was twenty-one years old. Born in England, she had gone to a shorthand typing college immediately after she had left school. Once she was qualified she took a position as a typist in Liverpool before turning her hand to teaching the skills necessary to be a good secretary. It was whilst she was teaching that she discovered a love for the stage and began to take small parts in various shows in and around Liverpool.

At the time, Gay lived with her mother in Bebington Road, Rock Ferry, Birkenhead, but when the war broke out in 1939, she joined ENSA and began working on shows for the serving

The Durban Castle, *the ship on which Gay Gibson met her death at the hands of James Camb.*

troops. She spent some time in the Intelligence Corps and, after hostilities were over, she travelled out to Johannesburg where her acting career blossomed. Now it was time to return to England where there were more opportunities for an up and coming actress.

It was the custom for first-class passengers to dine in small groups and Gay found herself sharing a table with Frank William Montague Hopwood and Wing Commander Bray. She spent a good deal of time in the company of these two gentlemen but appeared to be especially close to Mr Hopwood.

Exactly one week after the ship had sailed: Friday 17 October, the three friends dined together as usual after which they all adjourned to the lounge where Gay had three dances. At 11.00pm, or a few minutes later, Gay left the two gentlemen but joined them again in the smoke room at 11.30pm. They talked together until midnight before taking a stroll on the promenade deck where they stayed until around 12.35am on the Saturday, 18 October. All three then walked to B deck where the Wing Commander bade the other two goodnight. Frank Hopwood then escorted Gay back to cabin 126 where they spent a few minutes in conversation before Frank retired for the night to

A layout of the cabins on the Durban Castle. *Miss Gibson was killed in Cabin 126 and her body shoved out of the porthole.*

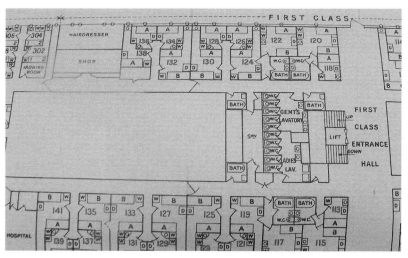

his own cabin, on C deck. Hopwood, Bray and other witnesses would all recall that Gay had been wearing a long black dress that evening.

Frederick Dennis Steer was one of the nightwatchmen on the ship. At around 3.00am, Steer heard the sound of bells ringing. Each cabin on board the ship had two buttons; one red and one green. Passengers could summon either a steward or a stewardess by pressing the appropriate button and this would cause the corresponding coloured light outside the cabin door to illuminate. It would also ring a bell and light up a button in the pantry, where the night staff spent the evening.

Going to his console, Steer saw that someone in cabin 126 had pressed both buttons and had, apparently, kept their finger on those buttons for the bells were ringing continuously. Steer, who was on Deck A at the time, made his way to cabin 126, which took him no more than four or five minutes.

Arriving at cabin 126, Steer saw that, as he had expected, both lights outside were illuminated. He knocked on the door but there was no reply. Fearful that the passenger inside might be in some distress, Steer pushed on the door and found that it was unlocked.

The lights were on inside the cabin but as the door swung slowly open, Steer caught a glimpse of a face he thought he recognised – James Camb. The man was standing to the left and he was wearing a white singlet with shoulder straps and a pair of black or blue trousers. Camb said: 'It's all right' and then pushed the door closed in Steer's face. Steer assumed that Camb, a steward, had heard the summons himself and was now attending to the cabin's occupant. However, Steer was also aware that Camb shouldn't really be in first-class so, rather puzzled, Steer took his story to his immediate boss who would still be in the pantry on A deck.

James Alfred Murray was the senior nightwatchman and he listened patiently as Steer told him what he believed he had just seen. Both men then returned to cabin 126 and listened outside. They could hear nothing and then, as Steer went about his duties, Murray stayed at the end of the passageway for close on ten minutes before going up to the Bridge to report the matter to the ship's captain.

Acting on the captain's instructions, Murray returned to cabin 126 and knocked again. There was still no answer but now Murray opened the door. The room was in total darkness and there was no sign of the cabin's occupant, Gay Gibson. Still, there was a possibility that she had merely gone for a stroll on the deck. For the time being, the matter was left to rest.

At 7.30am on 18 October, Eileen Elizabeth Field, the stewardess in charge of cabin 126, knocked on the door to see if Miss Gibson required anything. There was no reply so Eileen turned the handle. To her surprise, the door opened. Over the past week, she had always had to wait until Miss Gibson opened the door for her. There was also the concern that the room was a little more untidy than usual and the porthole was wide open.

Eileen began to tidy up but then suddenly realised that a pair of black silk pyjamas and a yellow flowered dressing gown were missing. Miss Gibson normally slept in the pyjamas and she certainly would not have gone for an early morning walk dressed in such attire. The matter was reported and in due course came to the attention of the captain again. Fearful that Miss Gibson might have fallen overboard, the ship was turned around and a search made.

The watch was doubled and a radio message was sent out to all ships in the area but by 11.40am, no sign of the missing passenger had been found. The captain, Arthur George Victor Patey, ordered that the ship return to its original course and a full enquiry was then launched.

As part of that enquiry, James Camb was interviewed. Patey told him that a man resembling him had been seen in cabin 126 at about 3.00am on the morning Miss Gibson had gone missing. Camb said that this could not have been him as he had never been in any passenger's cabin since he had finished work for the night at 12.45am.

Other interviews were conducted and in the course of these, it came to Captain Patey's attention that Camb had started wearing a long-sleeved jacket. The ship was in tropical waters at the time and in this heat, all the rest of the staff were dressed in short-sleeved tunics. When it was reported that Camb was sporting what looked like fresh scratches and might be wearing the jacket to conceal them, Captain Patey ordered that Camb be examined by the ship's surgeon and this took place the following day, 19 October. That same day, a fresh Yale lock was placed on the door of cabin 126 and the key then locked in the captain's safe. The matter would now be dealt with by the police, once the ship docked in Southampton. A radio message was sent ahead to inform the authorities what had occurred.

The ship docked at Southampton on Saturday, 25 October 1947 where it was met by Detective Sergeant John Quinlan, Detective Sergeant John Trevor Jones and Detective Constable Minden Plumley. Again, a number of people were interviewed until, finally, Sergeant Quinlan and Constable Minden spoke to James Camb.

Quinlan asked Camb if he had any explanation for Gay Gibson's disappearance adding that if he knew anything at all, now was the time to volunteer it. Rather surprisingly, Camb replied: 'You mean that Miss Gibson might have died from a cause other than being murdered. She might have had an attack or something?' He then went on to make a full statement.

In that document, Camb stated that Miss Gibson had invited him to her cabin and he had taken a drink for her. He noticed that she was wearing a nightgown with nothing underneath and, when she removed this, he climbed into bed beside her. They had intercourse together and, during the act, she suddenly stiffened and then went limp. He got out of bed and saw that she was frothing at the mouth and only one of her eyes was open.

Camb tried to give Miss Gibson artificial respiration and it was at this point that the nightwatchman, James Murray, knocked on the door. Once he had told Frederick Steer that everything was all right and he had been left alone again, Camb returned to the bed to find that there were no signs of life. Panicking over what people would think and the position he would be in, he lifted her limp body to the porthole and threw her out into the sea. He added that when it hit the water, the body made; '. . . a hell of a splash'.

Satisfied that Camb was actually responsible for Gay Gibson's death, Sergeant Quinlan then charged him with murder. After various police court appearances, Camb faced his trial for murder, at Winchester on 18 March 1948, before Mister Justice Hilbery. The case for the prosecution lay in the hands of Mr G D Roberts, whilst Camb was defended by Mr J D Casswell. The proceedings would last for four days.

Frank Hopwood, who had eaten at the same table as Gay Gibson, told the court that he was the victualling superintendent for the Union Castle line and had shared a table with her and Wing Commander Bray. During her time on the ship, Miss Gibson had only taken alcohol in moderation and, at the end of the meal on 17 October, she only had coffee to drink. He then confirmed that she was alive and well when he left her in her cabin during the early hours of 18 October.

William Albert Gravenor Pott was, like Camb, a steward on the ship and shared a cabin with him. He recalled seeing Camb in the deck pantry on D deck on 17 October. Camb was washing some glasses and Pott asked him if he needed a hand. Camb replied that he could manage. It was then some time around 12.30am and soon afterwards, Pott had gone up to the promenade deck and seen Miss Gibson standing between Mr Hopwood and Mr Bray, looking over the rail. Soon afterwards Pott retired to his cabin on A deck and was soon asleep. He woke at 6.00am and at that time, Camb was in his own bunk but Pott had not heard him come in. From that day onwards, Camb began wearing his long-sleeved white coat.

William Allan Conway was the boatswain's mate on the *Durban Castle* and during the period in question, his hours of duty were midnight until 4.00am. It was around 1.00am on 18 October when he walked onto the promenade deck. Miss Gibson was standing alone, near the rail, smoking a cigarette. Conway recalled that she was wearing a black dress. The decks were being swabbed down at the time and he warned her that she might get wet if she stayed where she was. He then saw her walk away, in the direction of cabin 126.

That afternoon, once it was public knowledge that Miss Gibson was missing, he had spoken to Camb and asked him when he had last seen her. Camb had remarked that it had been around 12.30am when she was with two gentlemen on that same promenade deck.

Frederick Steer told the court his story of the bells ringing in cabin 126 and of his attendance there. Some two or three days later, Camb had approached him and asked him if he were the person who had told the captain that he had been in Miss Gibson's cabin. Steer, acting on orders he had received from his superiors, replied that he had not and Camb then remarked: 'I am in a tight jam sir. Thank goodness I haven't been with her this trip.'

James Murray also referred to the incident of the bells ringing from cabin 126 but was also able to tell the court of an earlier incident. On the previous night, the Friday, he had been in the Long Gallery on D deck and heard Camb say to Miss Gibson: 'I have a bone to pick with you, and a big one at that.' Murray was astounded that a steward should be so familiar with any passenger, let alone a first-class one.

Eileen Field, who had been in charge of cabin 126 said that a few days before Miss Gibson vanished, she had seen Camb in the Long Gallery. At the time, Eileen was taking a tray to cabin 126 but Camb stopped her and volunteered the information that Miss Gibson was supposed to be three months pregnant, by a married man and added that she had told him herself. Eileen was most shocked to here Camb talk of a passenger in this way.

Continuing her testimony, Eileen said that she had last seen Miss Gibson at some time after 6.30pm on 17 October. On 25 October, when the police came aboard and wanted to examine the cabin she, acting on their instructions, had returned to cabin 126 and attempted to put things back where they had been before she had started tidying up. This said rather little for the existing idea of crime scene preservation!

Dr Anthony John Martin Griffiths was the surgeon on board the ship and on 19 October, acting on the captain's instructions, he had examined Camb. Dr Grifiths found several superficial scratches on Camb's left shoulder about one inch in length, which looked like they might have been made with fingernails. There were also several scratches on Camb's wrists that had again been recently inflicted. When asked to explain them, Camb said that he had woken up one morning with a terrible itch and must have scratched himself until he bled. As for the scratches on his shoulder, he had used a very rough towel and that might well have caused them.

Sergeant Quinlan told of his initial interview with Camb, which had taken place in the ship's Smoke Room. He began by saying that he was investigating Miss Gibson's disappearance to which Camb replied: 'Should I know anything about it?'

To further questions Camb said: 'I knew Miss Gibson. I have seen her on the deck and have attended to her.' He was then asked if he had ever been inside her cabin and answered: 'Never.' By then, Quinlan had discovered that it had been Camb's habit to serve Miss Gibson afternoon tea in her cabin but when pressed on this point, Camb retorted: 'Yes, but I was stopped from doing it. I only went there once or twice at the beginning of the trip.'

Camb was then asked about his whereabouts on the night of 17 October. He said that he had finished his duties and then gone on deck to have a smoke. He was in bed and asleep by 2.00am. The sighting of him in her cabin at 3.00am was then mentioned to which Camb would only comment: 'That's put me in a tight spot.'

Other police officers had been involved in the investigation. Sergeant John Trevor Addis had visited the ship on 25 October where he saw a palm print on the back of the door in cabin 126. He had photographed this and other parts of the cabin. He had also taken pictures of the scratches on Camb's wrists and shoulder.

Detective Chief Inspector Sidney Birch was in charge of the fingerprint department at New Scotland Yard and he had compared the palm print found on the cabin door with Camb's prints. They were identical showing that he had indeed been in cabin 126. The palm print was of course explained by the suggestion that this is where he had pushed the door closed on Frederick Steer.

Fibres had been found around the open port-hole in the cabin and stains had been seen on the bed sheets. These had been examined by Walter Eric Montgomery at the Metropolitan Police Laboratory at Hendon. He reported that he had found lipstick and tea stains on the pillow. There was brown boot polish on the counterpane and human bloodstains on the sheets.

These bloodstains had been tested by Dr Donald Teare and he said that they were type O. Camb had been tested and his blood was found to be of type A, showing that the blood belonged to someone else and almost certainly was Miss Gibson's. Perhaps more important was the finding of urine stains by Dr Teare for he stated that the involuntary evacuation of the bladder was quite common in cases of strangulation.

The jury were out for just forty-five minutes before returning their guilty verdict and Camb was sentenced to death. An appeal was entered but even before that was heard, the death sentence was commuted to one of life imprisonment. During this early part of 1948, capital punishment was being discussed at length and a clause, which would abolish hanging, was included in the new Criminal Justice Bill for discussion in the House of Commons. In the event, the House of Lords would reject this bill but in the meantime, all death sentences were commuted as a matter of course. Camb heard the news of his reprieve on 6 May.

Only after Camb's death sentence had been quashed did other witnesses come forward to tell their stories. Several women said that Camb had attacked them sexually during previous voyages on the *Durban Castle* and two claimed that he had actually raped them. One woman, Laura Daisy Annie Temple, even said that when she resisted, Camb had tried to strangle her.

Laura had left Southampton for Capetown on the *Durban Castle* on 11 September 1947, just about one month before the ship left on the fateful return journey on which Miss Gibson sailed. Laura had travelled with a Mrs Thompson and her two children and together the party had occupied cabins 104 and 106. During the early part of the voyage, Laura had spoken to Camb several times and they had become quite friendly.

On 18 September, Laura had gone out with Camb during the evening and at one stage had gone voluntarily with him into one of the cabins where deck equipment was kept. They had a drink together and then Camb locked the door and they sat down in two deck chairs. At this stage Camb asked Laura for a kiss and when she refused he attacked her, forced her into a kneeling position on one of the chairs and attempted to strangle her.

Fortunately, she passed out before he could complete the act and when she woke, he was standing over her, smiling. The evidence of Laura and the other ladies, seemed to underline that Camb was a sexual predator who was quite prepared to use violence to get what he wanted. In the case of Gay Gibson he had just gone too far.

Camb began his prison sentence and was eventually given parole in 1959. Seeking a new start in life he changed his surname to Clarke and obtained employment as a waiter. Unfortunately it was not the end of his criminal career for in May 1967 he was convicted of sexually attacking a thirteen-year-old girl, for which he was merely given probation. He then moved to Scotland where he worked in a restaurant but was then accused of sexual misconduct with three more schoolgirls. His parole was revoked and Camb was sent back to prison. Finally released in 1978, he died the following year.

Chapter 8

The Knobkerrie
Michael George Tatum
1959

Charles Frederick Barrett, a veteran of the Boer War, lived at 11 Belmont Road, Portswood, Southampton. The house had no fewer than eight rooms and Barrett occupied the front rooms on both the ground floor and the first floor. Other rooms had been let out to lodgers. Thus, John Gerrard Finn had a central room at the back on the first floor and the middle room downstairs. There was one other adult living at 11 Belmont Road, the housekeeper, Mrs Mary Tatum, who had moved in with her husband and baby daughter, three weeks before Christmas 1958. Since that time, Mr and Mrs Tatum had argued and, as a result, he had moved out in early January 1959, leaving Mary alone with her child.

John Finn worked nights and on the evening of Thursday, 15 January, he left for work at 7.00pm. He returned to Belmont Road at around 7.30am the following morning and entered the house through the back door, something he did as a matter of course. He could see immediately that something was wrong.

The conservatory door and window were open. Barrett was a creature of habit and always locked up the house at around 10.00pm each night, even turning off the water supply. For security purposes, the most he would ever leave unlocked was a small ventilation window.

As Finn walked further into the house he heard what he thought were snoring noises, coming from the direction of the hallway. Having first turned the water back on, Finn walked down the hallway and noticed that the door to the middle room, his own living room, was open.

Going upstairs to investigate further, Finn saw that Barrett's bedroom door was wide open and his light was on. Finn entered the room and saw, to his horror, a large round patch of blood in the centre of Barrett's pillow on the bed. As for Charles Barrett himself, he lay on the floor at the foot of the bed with his head towards the bed. He had a terrible gash on his forehead,

The bedroom at 11 Belmont Road, where Charles Frederick Barrett was attacked. Note the bloodstained items on the floor.

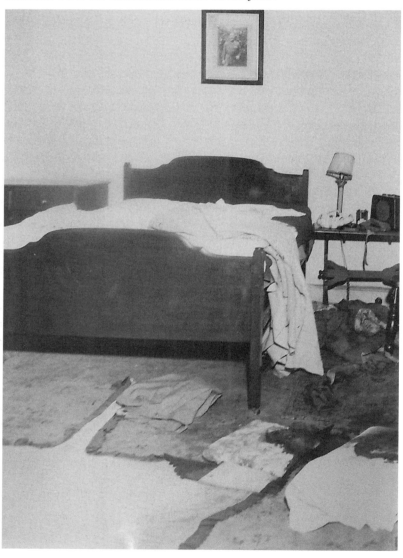

was covered in blood and made horrible choking and snoring noises. Barrett was still alive and Finn now had to summon help urgently. He dashed to Mrs Tatum's room and told her what he had found before running to the nearest public telephone box and calling for the police and an ambulance.

Finn waited at the telephone box for the police to arrive. The first officer on the scene was Constable Anthony John Bushrod. He went to the house with Finn and timed his arrival at 7.52am. Going into the bedroom where Barrett lay, Bushrod saw that the Venetian blinds were drawn. Barrett lay face down, in a large pool of blood and the top half of his body was saturated in the crimson liquid. He was wearing nothing but a shirt and it was difficult to determine exactly what injuries he had sustained. Gently, Constable Bushrod turned the injured man onto his side, rested his head on two pillows, which he took from the bed and placed some blankets over him to keep him warm until medical help arrived.

Bushrod noticed that when he had first entered the room, the bedclothes had been pulled back and one of the pillows was heavily bloodstained. This suggested that the initial attack had taken place whilst Barrett was in bed, possibly asleep. Had he disturbed an intruder, been struck once and then leapt out of bed to confront the assailant whereupon he had been attacked again?

In due course the ambulance arrived and Barrett was rushed to hospital. Constable Bushrod accompanied the injured man and noted, as he left the house, that there were a large number of African weapons displayed on the wall in the hallway. There was a mark on the wall where one weapon was missing from that display.

In fact, the weapon used to batter Charles Barrett was, to say the least, a most

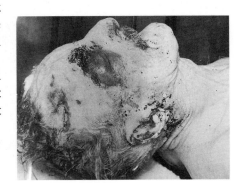

The body of Charles Barrett, showing the injuries he had sustained on his head.

unusual one. Barrett was a collector of African artefacts and one item he owned was a knobkerrie, which was basically a long, rather springy stick with a heavy, ball-shaped head. This had been given to Barratt by H Ryder Haggard, the author of many adventure stories including *King Solomon's Mines* and *She*. The knobkerrie was used by swinging it at an adversary, and the spring in the shaft would add to the momentum of the heavy head, thus adding to its impact. It was this weapon which had been taken from the wall display and used to attack Charles Barrett.

Despite receiving prompt medical attention, Charles Barrett died from his injuries at 10.30am that same day. This was now a case of murder and, further, it was a case of capital murder.

In 1957, the Homicide Act had come into force. Prior to this, the mandatory sentence for murder was death by hanging but the law had now changed. Now, a murderer would only face the noose if his crime fell in to one of five categories. These categories were: murder in the furtherance of theft, murder by shooting or explosion, murder whilst resisting arrest or during an escape, murder of a police officer or prison officer and two murders committed on different occasion. Since the house was ransacked, it appeared that robbery had been the motive in this crime. If that was indeed shown to be the case, then the killer, when he was caught, would face the death penalty.

Two factors immediately caused the police to surmise that this crime had been committed by someone who knew the house well. To begin with, there was no sign of a forced entry. The assailant had either been let in by his victim or had a key to the premises. Further, the weapon had been taken down from the wall, implying that the miscreant had known of its existence. It was this line of argument which led officers to twenty-four-year-old Michael George Tatum who had only left his wife and moved out of the house a week or so ago. The first step for the police was to find out what they could about Tatum.

Officers soon discovered that Tatum had left school at the age of sixteen and a number of jobs had followed, mainly as a cinema projectionist, but he had found the late nights rather too much and had finally sought other employment. A native of London he had met his future wife, Mary Theresa, in September 1956. They married the following year and lived together at 103 Frithfield Gardens in Shepherd's Bush. On 12 February 1958, the couple had had a daughter, Yvonne, and soon afterwards, in the following November, the family had decided that they needed a fresh start and decided to move to Southampton where Mary's brother lived.

For two weeks, the Tatums had lived at 107 Mansell Road until Mary saw an advertisement in the local newspaper from a gentleman seeking a housekeeper. In return for light household duties, a free flat would be provided. That led Mary to an interview with Charles Barrett and a move to 11 Belmont Road. At about the same time, Michael got a job as a fitter for Firestone Tyres and things appeared to be improving for the family.

On 5 January 1959, Michael Tatum had taken five shillings from his wife's purse and gone out for a drink. When he returned, he had argued with his wife not only about the money he had taken but also about the fact that he expressed a desire to purchase a car at a time they could ill afford it. For the rest of that week, the couple did not speak to each other. Things went from bad to worse when Michael Tatum returned home from work early on Friday 9 January and informed his wife that he had been dismissed, as his references had been unsatisfactory. He handed over £4 in cash and told her that it would be better for her if she returned to Scotland where she had once lived. As a result of that, Mary had spoken to Mr Barrett and told him that she was thinking of leaving. He asked her to stay and said that he would speak to her husband and ask him to leave the house instead. Mary did move out for a few days, and went back to her brother's house but did eventually return. As for her husband, he had packed his belongings and moved out of Belmont Road at 1.00pm on Saturday, 10 January, just five days before the attack upon Mr Barrett. It was now time for officers to interview their suspect.

At 2.45pm that same day, Detective Inspector Robert John Masters, Detective Sergeant Harry Ancill and Detective Sergeant Patrick Joseph O'Sullivan were in Tennyson Road when they saw a man fitting Tatum's description approaching them. Ancill identified himself as a police officer and asked the man if he were Michael George Tatum. The man said that he was, whereupon he was informed that the officers were investigating an incident in which serious injuries had been inflicted upon Mr Barrett. At this stage, the officers did not reveal that Barrett had died from his injuries and that they were investigating something much more serious than an assault. Tatum was asked if he would answer some questions about his movements of the previous evening. Tatum said he knew nothing about the matter but agreed to go to the police station to offer what help he could.

Once at the station, Tatum was asked to empty his pockets and amongst the items he produced was a wallet containing £7 in one pound notes. There was also a key case, which held two keys and Tatum confirmed that one was the key to the house at 11 Belmont Road. The other was the key to his new lodgings. Asked now to confirm his movements of the previous night Tatum said that he had been out with two friends, Trevor and Don.

According to Tatum's statement, he had met Trevor and Don in The Oak public house at the bottom of Cambridge Road and was with them from around 8.00pm until 9.45pm. He had then left them and gone alone to another pub, at the other end of Cambridge Road, where he had stayed until closing time. He had then left, with a 'chap' he had met in there and went with him to his flat where he stayed until around 12.45am. He had never seen this man before but he gave the name Derek and they had driven to Derek's ground floor flat in a fawn coloured Zephyr or possibly a Zodiac.

Some time after this, whilst the initial story was being checked out, Tatum confided to Inspector Masters that this Derek had given him £8 in cash for 'future promises'. The suggestion was that Derek was a homosexual and Tatum had led him on, promising to go back to his flat on the Sunday. Tatum of course had no intention of returning and in fact, couldn't say precisely where the flat was, though he could show the officers the street it was on.

At 9.00pm, Tatum was interviewed again and asked if he were sure that the statement he had given was correct. Tatum said that it was but added that when he left Derek's flat he had been given a lift back to the end of Cambridge Road. He then gave a description of Derek as six feet tall, aged about 30, with fair, wavy hair and wearing a brown suit. Tatum had also noticed a pair of string driving gloves in the car.

Tatum was now asked to provide more details of the two men he had spent the earlier part of the evening with, Trevor and Don. He said he had met them in the public bar of *The Oak* but didn't know their surnames. He had known them only by sight and had been in other bars with them on previous occasions. He was then asked to draw the layout of the bar where they had all met up and it was noticed that Tatum drew the plan with his left hand. This was significant because by now, medical evidence had suggested that the killer was almost certainly left-handed.

Inspector Masters decided that it was time to check out Tatum's alibi. Again accompanied by Ancill and O'Sullivan, Masters drove Tatum to Cambridge Road, to positively identify the two pubs and to try to trace Derek's house.

The first pub, *The Oak*, did not exist. Tatum explained that the pub he had been in had a sign outside with a tree on it. The only establishment that might have fitted that description was the *Royal Oak* in Ledger Road and Tatum confirmed that this was the one he meant. Immediately, the licensee, Reginald Cole was brought across to the car and asked if Tatum had been in there the previous night. Cole said that he hadn't but Cole's wife, Gladys, said she believed she remembered him being there.

The car was driven on in an attempt to find the second pub, the one in which Tatum said he had met Derek. After some driving around, Tatum finally identified the *Waggoners Arms* as the correct one. Once again the licensee, Mrs Brooking, was asked if she could identify Tatum as a customer of hers. She stated that he had not been in her pub the previous night. She was quite sure, as there had only been four customers all night. One of those was a regular named Mitchell and he too confirmed that Tatum had not been in the *Waggoners Arms*.

Tatum said that he must have been mistaken and soon picked out another pub, the *Red Lion*. Here Edmund Dollery, the licensee, was asked to identify Tatum but he too said he had not been in the previous evening. A search was now made for Derek's flat, but Tatum failed to pick out the road where it was. He was then driven back to the police station for further questioning.

Back at the station, Inspector Masters said it was obvious that Tatum was lying. Only Gladys Cole had been able to say that she might have seen him. Added to that, he had a key to Charles Barrett's house and, since there had been no forced entry, the assailant must have had a key. Tatum thought for a few moments then apologised for lying and said that he had done so because he was shielding someone. He now wished to make another statement.

According to this new statement, Tatum maintained that he had indeed met Trevor and Don but had originally lied to keep them out of it. The three men had been to the Bargate area together and afterwards they had all gone to Don's where they stayed until 2.30am. Later, as Tatum had been leaving he had seen the Derek he referred to in his earlier statement, relieving himself against his car outside the *Gordon Arms*. After that, the rest of the original statement had been true.

Tatum did give a little more information however. He now revealed that Don's surname was Russell and he lodged with Don's parents, almost opposite the *Gordon Arms* which was on Portswood Road. His house had a yellow door.

Inspector Masters now drove to Portswood Road where he did find a house with a yellow door – number 96. This was the address of both Trevor Tughill and Keith Donald Russell. Statements were taken from both men and, on his return to the police station, Masters informed Tatum that he would be detained pending further enquiries.

The following day, Tatum was informed that Charles Barrett had died and this was now a case of murder. Tatum asked for time to think and then said he wished to make another statement. In this third document he admitted that after leaving Trevor and Don he had met up with a man he knew and during the subsequent conversation, Tatum had mentioned that he hadn't seen his wife since the previous Saturday. He suggested that they both go round to Belmont Road to visit her.

Using his key, Tatum opened the front door and both men went inside. The house was all quiet and Tatum's friend had a fountain pen type torch which he used to light his way upstairs after first taking the knobkerrie off the wall. The man went into Barrett's bedroom and stole a wallet from the table by the bed. At this point Barrett sat up and Tatum headed for the door as his friend struck out with the weapon. They both then ran from the house and divided the money up once they had made good their escape. Tatum refused to name this friend, preferring he said to take the blame himself as he was the cause of all the trouble. Later that same day, Tatum was charged with capital murder.

Tatum had claimed that after taking the money out, he had disposed of Barrett's wallet in a hedge. At 10.15am on 18 January, Sergeant Ancill found the wallet in Spring Crescent. It could be proved that this had belonged to Barrett as it contained a receipt for £250 of Premium Bonds, which Barrett had purchased. Tatum was now interviewed again and finally admitted that the man with him, the one who had actually struck the fatal blow, was one Terry Thatcher and he lived in St Mary's Road but he did not know the number of the house.

Tatum was asked to give more details on the mysterious Mr Thatcher and said that they had first met at a pub in Millbrook Road about one week after Tatum had first arrived in Southampton. Two weeks before the attack upon Barrett, Tatum had seen Thatcher at the Labour Exchange as he too was now looking for work.

Once again Inspector Masters tried to check Tatum's story. The Labour Exchange said they had no Terry Thatcher on their books and no trace of such a man could be found anywhere around the St Mary's Road area. In fact, no person by the name of Terry Thatcher could be found anywhere in Southampton. The conclusion was that Tatum had spun one lie after another in order to avoid the consequences of his actions and the police now believed that he had acted alone.

Twenty-four-year-old Michael George Tatum appeared before Mister Justice Cassels at Winchester on 19 March 1959. The trial lasted until 23 March and during that time, the case for the Crown was led by Mr Norman Skelhorn who was assisted by Mr Jeremy Hutchinson. Tatum was defended by Mr E S Fay, assisted by Mr Patrick Back.

John Finn, the lodger at 11 Belmont Road, told the court that Charles Barrett had been quite security conscious. In addition to locking up the house each night, he never left windows open except for the small ventilation window which was sometimes left open a couple of inches. Finn also confirmed that it was his habit to pay the rent for his rooms each Saturday morning. Barrett always put the cash straight into his wallet and Finn identified the wallet Sergeant Ancill had found as identical to the one Barrett had owned. Finally, Finn was able to say that Tatum knew that he worked nights and that only Barrett and Mrs Tatum would be in the house.

Dr Robert Kenneth Jackson was the house surgeon at the Royal Hants Hospital. He had examined Charles Barrett, at 9.00am on 16 January. Barrett was unconscious and almost exsanguinated. He bore a Y-shaped lacerated wound on his right forehead and had a depressed skull fracture. There was also a small, lacerated wound behind the right ear. Barrett was given a blood transfusion but remained unconscious. His condition deteriorated steadily until he finally died.

Dr Richard Anthony Goodbody was a consultant pathologist and he performed the post-mortem on Barrett. He confirmed the wounds detailed by Dr Jackson and added that he had found an extensive depressed fracture of the right parietal, frontal and temporal bones. These had been caused by at least three blows from a blunt instrument. Dr Goodbody also stated that if Barrett had been sitting up in bed at the time of the attack, as stated by Tatum in his final statement, then the blows would have been inflicted by a left handed man. However, it was possible that they might also have been caused by a back-handed blow from a right-handed man. The injuries observed were consistent with the use of the knobkerrie, found broken into three pieces, at the scene.

Mrs Joan Mary Ware had made the formal identification of Charles Barrett's body. Joan was a widow and the daughter of the dead man. She had last visited her father the previous winter and at that time he had been in good health.

After the attack, Dennis Charles Barrett, the dead man's son, had been taken to the house in Belmont Road by Inspector Masters. The safe was opened and whilst Dennis was present, Inspector Masters took possession of £250 of Premium Bonds. The numbers were the same as those written on the back of the receipt found in the wallet in Spring Crescent: WB 222001 to 222200 and PB 288751 to 288800. Further, Dennis was able to say that the numbers had been written in his father's hand.

Gladys May Cole was the wife of the licensee of the *Royal Oak* and on 16 January she had said that she believed Tatum was in her pub on the night Charles Barrett was attacked. Gladys had now retracted that and now testified that she did not think she had seen Tatum on the night in question. However, the Trevor and Don that Tatum had referred to had both made statements admitting that they had indeed met up with him.

Trevor Graham Toughill lived at 96 Portswood Road and on 5 January, he had been in the *Gordon Arms* when he met 'Mike', the name by which he knew Tatum. Trevor was a lodger at Dons parent's house and he now confirmed that all three of them had been out for a drink on 5 January. Mike had told them that he was in the Australian navy and was a single man. On 15 January, the three new friends went out to a number of pubs including the *Gordon Arms* and the *Belmont Hotel*, which they left at 8.30pm. They caught a bus into town and on that journey, Mike admitted that he was broke. He borrowed some money off Don, saying that he would pay him back on Friday, when he got his wages. The three men had a drink in town before returning to the *Gordon Arms* where they arrived in time for last orders. All three then went back to Portswood Road and Mike left at around 11.35pm.

The next morning, 16 January, Mike returned to Don's house at 10.20am and returned the £1 he had borrowed the night before. Trevor and Mike then went to the *Gordon Arms* again at which point Mike, maintaining the idea that he was in the Australian navy, said that he had exchanged some currency and was disappointed with the rate he had received. Mike then pulled out a wallet, which Trevor now said looked very much like the one produced as an exhibit in court; the one identified as belonging to the dead man.

Later that day, Mike had asked if he might borrow a brown suit, though he gave no reason for this request. Trevor was also able to say that Mike had never mentioned meeting anyone else after he had left Don's house, nor had he ever mentioned anyone named Terry Thatcher.

The next witness was Keith Donald Russell, the Don in Tatum's story, and he backed up much of what Trevor Toughill had said. He was also able to confirm to the court that Mike was none other than the prisoner in the dock.

Trevor Turley lodged at 36 Cambridge Road and had shared his room with Tatum since the latter had left Belmont Road. Trevor had not known Tatum's surname and he too only knew him as Mike. He had been told, by Mike, that he was in the Australian navy.

On the evening of 15 January, Trevor had left his lodgings at 6.00pm. Mike was still there at the time but when Trevor returned home at 11.00pm, Mike was out. He was still out when Trevor went to bed. When he woke at 8.00am the next morning, Mike was in bed.

Edward Thomas Stacey worked at the Employment Exchange and he confirmed that there was no one registered with the name Terry Thatcher. Tatum was registered, from 3 December 1958 and had last signed on 17 December.

Eric Dermott Sweet was the Principal Scientific Officer at the Metropolitan Police laboratory at New Scotland Yard. On 17 January, he had received the knobkerrie, samples of the dead man's hair, and items of Tatum's clothing including a dark grey overcoat, a pair of trousers, and a pair of gloves.

The head of the knobkerrie was some three and three quarter inches long by two and a half inches thick. There were several bloodstains observed on the head but only a small amount on the part of the shaft that the assailant would have held. The weapon had broken in two places during the attack. Two human hairs had been found on the shaft, and these were similar to the samples removed from Charles Barrett after death. As for the clothing collected, no blood was found on any of the items, apart from the gloves. These appeared to have been dyed recently but traces of blood were found in the stitched seams.

In effect, Tatum's defence was two-fold. In the first place, it was claimed that he had not entered the house alone and that Terry Thatcher was the man who had struck the fatal blows. Tatum had had no idea that violence would be used. The second part of the defence was that Tatum was showing signs of schizophrenia and therefore had impaired mental responsibility. These two factors meant that he should be found guilty of manslaughter and not murder.

The first line of defence has already been mentioned. The local employment exchange had no record of a Terry Thatcher but the police were not prepared to let the matter rest there. A much wider net had been cast and a Terry Thatcher was, eventually, found, living in Chiswick, London. He testified that he did not know Tatum and had only ever been in Southampton once in his life. That was to a football match some eight years previously. Even Tatum had to admit that this was not the Terry Thatcher he claimed to have known.

Of more import, perhaps, was evidence called as to Tatum's mental state. The court heard that up to 1956, Tatum had been a good and conscientious worker but then, for no apparent reason, had started to tell lies. Dr Atkin testified that such episodes were symptomatic of the early stages of schizophrenia. Examples of these lies had already been given in court, when witnesses stated that Tatum had told them he was in the Australian navy. Other examples were also given. On one occasion, Tatum had visited a cinema projectionist in Kensington and told him he was a policeman. On other occasion, when he worked at the Renown Cinema in London he had failed to turn up for work one day and sent a messenger to tell his employer that his wife was very ill. Later, another message said that she had died. The staff organised a collection and purchased a wreath to show their sympathy and support when, a day or two later, Mrs Tatum walked in and asked for her husband's wages! Not surprisingly, Tatum was sacked.

In due course the jury retired to consider their verdict. They found that Tatum was guilty as charged and, since this was a capital crime, the only sentence possible was death by hanging. An appeal was entered against that sentence but this was dismissed on 27 April and Tatum's fate was sealed.

On Thursday, 14 May 1959, twenty-four-year-old Michael George Tatum was hanged at Winchester by Robert Leslie Stewart and Thomas Cunliffe. It was the fourth execution of the year and three more men would face a similar fate before the year was over.

Chapter 9

Cowboys and Indians
Keith Ridley
1960

Saturday, 20 February 1960 was a perfectly normal day in Mayfield Park, Southampton. There were three separate football matches taking place on the pitches and in all, around one hundred people cheered on the various teams. In the woods nearby, a group of eight or ten children were enjoying a game of Cowboys and Indians in an area known locally as Smuggler's Den.

Two of the children playing in the woods were thirteen-year-old Malcom Dawkins and his nine-year-old sister, Iris Margaret. The brother and sister were very close and Malcolm had even loaned Iris his precious Rustler Gem toy pistol so that she could join in. Then, suddenly, in the excitement of the game, Iris slipped and fell into a small stream. The little girl got her feet wet and some mud on her legs. With a sigh, she said she would have to go home to get changed. It was then around 4.00pm.

At around 4.45pm, Malcolm decided that it was about time he headed off for home too. Arriving at the family house at 7, Sparsholt Road, Weston, Malcolm naturally asked how Iris was and was surprised to hear that his parents had seen nothing of her. He explained about her accident and said that she had left the woods about forty-five minutes before and should have arrived home well before him.

Iris Dawkins was a shy girl and not one to talk to strangers. This immediately raised concerns with her parents, Percy and Maisie, who wasted no time in taking their concerns to officers at Bitterne police station. A search was organised and, at 11.00pm that night, Iris' body was found in Mayfield woods, a few hundred yards from where she had been playing her game.

Iris lay face downwards on a piece of boggy land and she had been stabbed repeatedly. The toy gun she had borrowed from her brother was found amongst the folds of her clothing. A later examination would show no less than thirty-nine stab wounds, of varying degrees of severity. It would also show that no sexual assault had taken place.

A public appeal was made for anyone who had been in the area of Mayfield Park that afternoon. A description of the clothing Iris had been wearing was also circulated and this informed the public that at the time she had met her death, the little girl had been dressed in a pale blue woollen jumper, dark blue jeans, black plimsolls and a white hat. Anyone who had seen a girl wearing those clothes was asked to contact the police without delay.

The response was all the investigating officers could have hoped for. By 22 February, two days after the murder, more than one hundred people who had been watching the football matches, playing in them, or just walking in the vicinity of the woods, had come forward. Most of them had seen nothing untoward but they were able to pass on descriptions of other people they had seen in the area.

Officers were drafted in to the enquiry and visited no less than fifteen local schools. The children were spoken to and asked to answer three questions. First, had they been in the park on the previous Saturday? Second, could they describe anyone they had seen there? Third, if they had already been interviewed by the police, had they thought of anything else since?

The funeral of the tragic victim took place at Weston Church in Weston Lane, at 3.30pm on Friday, 24 February. It was well attended and, in the meantime, it looked as if the police might well have got the breakthrough they so badly needed.

Malcolm Hughes was, like Iris, nine years old and he attended the same school as the dead girl. He had been a friend of hers and told officers about a 'big bully', a larger and older boy who had been in the woods a week before Iris had met her death. This boy, who Malcolm said was about thirteen or fourteen, had pushed Iris down a grassy bank in the woods and when Malcolm bravely went to help his friend, the boy had thrown a knife at him. Luckily the knife missed but the boy made it plain that if they spoke to anyone about what had happened, he would hurt them. Malcolm described the boy as being about five feet seven inches tall, with ginger or auburn hair. He had freckles on his face and a scratch near one eye. He was wearing a black leather jacket. Could it be that this bully had been in the woods the following week too? It was certainly someone the police needed to speak to.

Other people had also come forward to describe individuals they had seen in the woods on that fateful Saturday. Many of these people had, in their turn, also been traced, interviewed and eliminated but, by 26 February, the police had issued descriptions of two young men they wished to interview.

The first of these was the bully described by Malcolm Hughes but the second was a boy seen, at about 4.00pm, leaning against a tree on a wooden slope at the back of the goalposts near the Barnfield Road end of the park. This was only about forty yards from where Iris' body was later found. He was described as being about fifteen years old, had fair, untidy hair and a round face which was either dirty or muddy.

The following day, Saturday, 27 February, the game of Cowboys and Indians was reconstructed, in the hope that further memories would be jogged. A total of ten children were in the woods at the time; five who had been playing with Iris and five others who had come forward with some information about people they had seen in the area.

Still the investigation continued. On Monday, 29 February, a team of fifty police officers started making door to door enquiries in the Weston, Itchen and Woolston areas. It was on that day, as a result of those door to door interviews, that a ten year old boy came forward to say that he had seen Iris as she was heading home from her playmates.

This was a crucial statement for, up to this time, no one had been found who had seen Iris alive after she had parted from her brother and the other children. The boy was taken to the Bitterne police station on the afternoon of 29 February and given a room overnight so that he could be interviewed at length.

As a result of what this boy said, a report was prepared and sent to the Chief Constable of Southampton, Mr C G Box. He considered that report and then forwarded it on to the Director of Public Prosecutions. The report was digested and as a result, the boy who had come forward was arrested and charged with the murder of Iris Dawkins.

Throughout all the various legal proceedings and court appearances, the accused boy would never be formally identified to the public. In press reports he was always referred to by only his first name, which the court said could be revealed. So it was that on Monday, 21 March 1960, ten-year-old 'Jeffrey' made his first appearance before the magistrates, to be remanded for one week.

Various other remands followed until eventually Jeffrey was sent to face his trial at the next Wiltshire assizes, at Salisbury. They opened on 10 May and Jeffrey duly appeared before Mister Justice Pilcher who listened to legal arguments and then transferred to case to the Hampshire assizes which would open in July. After all, this had been a Hampshire crime and should be dealt with by the authorities in that county.

The case finally opened, at Winchester, on Tuesday, 12 July and again the judge in charge was Mister Justice Pilcher. The case for the Crown was led by Mr Peter Rawlinson, who was assisted by Mr A C Munro Kerr. Jeffrey's defence was led by Mr Norman Skelhorn, assisted by Mr Terence Read. The jury consisted of three women and nine men.

Details of the game the children had been playing, and of Iris' subsequent accident in the stream, were given not only by her brother, Malcolm, but also by Pamela Craddock and Russell Otto, two of the other children. They said that Iris had slipped and got her feet wet in the stream. She also had a little mud on her clothing and said she was going home to change. The last time any of them had seen her was when she headed off, towards her home in Sparsholt Road.

In the early part of the investigation, much import had been given to the story of the ginger-haired bully, related by Malcolm Hughes. Subsequent investigations had shown that Malcolm's entire story had been an invention. A number of young children had given false accounts to the police and it was surmised that they had not told tales out of malice but simply wanted their moment in the spotlight. They were, after all, only very young.

No charges were ever made against Malcolm Hughes or any of the other children who had made up stories.

The time came to give details of Jeffrey's involvement in the case. He and his family had first been interviewed on 26 February by Detective Constable Nicholson, as part of a door to door enquiry. The officer had seen Jeffrey in the presence of his mother and the boy had volunteered the information that he was in Mayfield Park on 20 February. Further, he admitted that he had a black leather jacket like that mentioned in one of the descriptions and added that he thought he might have seen Iris leaving the woods.

Constable Nicholson reported what Jeffrey had said and visited the house for a second time, again as part of the door to door investigations on 29 February. Now Jeffrey elaborated on his story saying that when he had seen Iris, he had also seen another boy close by. It was then that Jeffrey was escorted to Bitterne police station so that he could be formally interviewed. He was accompanied by his father and Jeffrey was there overnight, not leaving until 1 March.

During that interview, Jeffrey had talked of watching stabbings on television and added that it wasn't real because you could see someone killed in one episode but then next week they'd be back in another play. The conversation continued and Jeffrey then admitted that when he had been in the woods, he had had a knife with him. Further questioning had Jeffrey admit that he had asked Iris to play 'chase' with him and at one stage they had fallen together. He had his knife in his hand at the time and it might well have gone into Iris, but Jeffrey wasn't sure. Finally, he admitted that it might, after all, have gone into her more than once.

Jeffrey then made a full statement. He said that he had had a football with him and was kicking it about when it went into the woods. He went to retrieve it and saw Iris walking up the embankment. He described the chase game in detail and then added: 'When she fell over I fell on top of her and I think the knife went into her shoulder when I fell on her. Only a little though.'

'She was lying down and her eyes were open and she was breathing normally. I thought she was playing.'

Jeffrey's testimony did seem to fit with that of Hilda Rosemary Elizabeth Connis who had been in her kitchen at 84 Achery Grove, at around 4.00pm on 20 February. She had looked out of the window and seen a little girl, who may have been Iris, being chased by a boy wearing a black leather jacket.

On 8 March, Jeffrey had been interviewed for the final time, again at his home. Now he withdrew his statement, said that he hadn't seen Iris at all. He did play with a girl who looked a bit like Iris but he didn't have a knife with him at the time.

Medical evidence was given by Dr Richard Anthony Goodbody, the pathologist who had performed the post-mortem on Iris. He said that many of the thirty-nine wounds inflicted upon Iris were superficial and some were obviously defence wounds. There were three serious wounds, any one of which might have caused death and some of the other wounds appeared to have been inflicted after death.

There were, however, problems with Jeffrey's admission to killing Iris. He had described her clothing as different to the items she was actually wearing. He also said that he met her coming from a certain direction when all the evidence pointed to her having walked directly from the woods towards her home. The various medical witnesses could not agree on a precise time of death with opinion now saying that Iris could have been killed as late as 9.30pm that night. Finally, there were the many examples, including the 'evidence' of Malcolm Hughes, of children who had invented stories about the murder.

On the second day of the trial Mr Justice Pilcher ruled that there was not sufficient evidence that could be given to a jury. In addition to the doubts already mentioned, no blood had been found on any items of Jeffrey's clothing. It was simply not safe to continue and consequently, the jury was instructed to return a not guilty verdict. Jeffrey was free to return to his family and the case remained on file as an unsolved murder. The years passed and no more was heard about the tragic death of Iris Dawkins until one day in November 1968.

Constable Dennis Arthur Luty was a member of the Southampton Vice Squad but on Monday, 18 November, he was off duty and taking Sophie, his Doberman Pinscher dog, for a walk in Mayfield woods. At one stage the dog froze and began growling and barking at a particular part of the bushes. Luty could see that there was something or someone in the bushes but before he could investigate, a man emerged and walked away.

Curious, Luty followed the man and saw him walk into Archery Road where he began stopping at various houses, apparently taking a very keen interest in them. Constable Luty now noticed that the man was wearing rubber gloves and felt that he might be considering breaking in to one of the homes. Luty moved forward, identified himself as a police officer and searched the man. He was carrying a large sheath knife and on the strength of that, and his previous rather strange behaviour, Luty arrested the man on suspicion and took him in for questioning.

At the police station the man, who identified himself as twenty-two-year-old Keith Ridley, was asked about being in the Mayfield park area. He admitted that he was waiting for someone in the hope of stealing their wallet but then immediately changed his story. With the comment: 'No, I had better tell you the truth.' Ridley then went on to admit his part in the murder of Iris Dawkins eight years before.

Ridley continued: 'I get the urge to kill every so often. I had bought the knife and came out with the intention of killing someone.'

'I'll tell you now, I killed someone in Mayfield Park about ten years ago. Her name was Iris Dawkins.'

'I stabbed a girl a long time ago, a little way in the bushes. Every so often I get the urge to kill somebody. Now you have got me. I thought it best to tell you about it and then I can't kill anyone else.'

In his written statement, Ridley went on to say that he had seen the children playing by the stream. He watched them for a while and then saw a girl leave the others and walk towards him, in the direction of the football pitches. As she drew near to him, Ridley grabbed her and forced her into the bushes at the point of a knife. Then he stabbed her in the back. He wasn't sure how many times he had actually stabbed her but stopped when he thought she was dead. Then she moved, and started screaming so he stabbed her some more times.

At the time of the attack upon Iris, Ridley himself had only been thirteen years old. He had then lived at 18 Laburnam Grove, Weston and explained to the police that after the murder, he had buried the knife near the back door of that address. A search of both that garden and of Mayfield woods was then organised, in which the Royal Engineers assisted, equipped with metal detectors but no knife was ever found.

Ridley also told officers about his own history. After leaving school he had found employment as a clerk in Southampton and had worked there until October 1968. He had then decided that he wanted a change and quit his job, moving to Northampton where he hoped to get a new job. He had no luck there and returned to his family in Peartree Avenue, on Friday 15 November.

Once again a report was sent to the Chief Constable and, once again it was forwarded on to the Director of Public Prosecutions. Finally, on 12 December, the newspapers carried reports that a man was to be charged with Iris' murder.

A number of remands followed with the last one taking place on 3 January 1969. It was after that hearing that Mr William Ackroyd, appearing for Ridley, made a public appeal for the widest possible publicity in this case. According to Mr Ackroyd, many of Ridley's old friends had since moved away from the Southampton area and he wanted anyone who had known his client at the time of the murder to get in touch with the defence.

Ridley's trial opened at Winchester on Monday, 17 March 1969 before Mister Justice Browne. Ridley was defended by Mr George Polson whilst the case for the prosecution was outlined by Sir Joseph Molony.

It was obvious that the defence would draw parallels with the earlier trial of Jeffrey. In both Jeffrey's case and Ridley's, the main strut of the prosecution was a confession. In neither case was a murder weapon found and the defence claimed that, just as Jeffrey's case was dismissed, so too should Ridley's. There was, though, more substantial circumstantial evidence on this occasion.

Ridley had given a very accurate description of the wounds inflicted upon Iris' body. Whilst the number of wounds had been detailed in past press reports, and descriptions of some wounds given, no article had ever mentioned that Iris had been stabbed twice in the throat. Ridley's statement did contain just such an admission.

The murder scene itself had also never been accurately described in the newspapers but Ridley's description was precise. On the day after his arrest he had been taken back to the woods and asked to show officers where the attack took place. Though the woods were very large, Ridley picked a spot just a few yards from the actual location.

There had also been many reports in the press that when she had fallen into the stream, Iris had slipped off a small bridge. Only Ridley's statement correctly identified this 'bridge' as a small tree which had fallen across the stream.

Witnesses were called from Ridley's family to try to show that he had not behaved strangely in any way after the attack upon Iris. His father, William said that Ridley had always been a truthful boy. His family had formed part of the door to door interviews in 1960 and Keith had told officers that he had not been near the woods on the day of the attack.

Mrs Daphne Woods, Keith Ridley's married sister said that her brother had always been a quiet boy and she did not notice the slightest change in his behaviour after Iris had been killed.

More telling, perhaps, was the testimony of Keith's brother, Terrence. He explained that in late 1959 he had found a sheath knife, which he often played with. One day, as he was leaving the house through the back garden he had stuck the knife into the door of their garden shed, intending to retrieve it later. When he did get home, the knife was missing so Terence had thrown the sheath away. Later, after Iris had been murdered, the police called at their house as part of their routine investigation and the officer had with him a sheath that they had found in the woods. Terence told them that this was the one he had thrown away. At the time, this was not seen as significant but it now appeared clear that Keith had been the one who took that knife and later used it upon Iris Dawkins.

Mister Justice Browne summed up the evidence on Wednesday, 26 March and the jury of ten men and two women retired to consider their verdict. In the event, they took just two and a half hours to determine that Keith Ridley was guilty as charged.

Since he had only been thirteen at the time of the murder, Ridley was sentenced to be detained during Her Majesty's pleasure. As he was taken from the dock to begin that sentence, Ridley broke down in tears. Finally, after eight long years, the motiveless murder of Iris Dawkins had been solved.

Chapter 10

Jekyll and Hyde
Dorothy Bray
1967

It was an all too familiar story to Edward Richard John Hockless and his wife, Edith Joyce, who preferred to use her second name. They had heard it all so many times before. Edward and Joyce lived at Flat 24, Robere House, Radstock Road, Southampton and opposite to them, at Flat 23, lived the Brays and they argued almost non-stop.

On Saturday, 3 June 1967, Edward and Joyce had been out for a few hours, only returning to their home at around 6.00pm. Even as they turned their key in the lock, they could hear the sounds of yet another argument coming from the Bray's house. Still, it was nothing to do with them so they closed the door of their flat and tried to ignore what was going on.

More difficult to ignore was the very loud bang that was heard at 6.40pm. At first, Edward Hockless believed that it might have been a car backfiring in the street outside but five minutes later, at 6.45pm, his front-door bell rang. In fact, the bell continued to ring for the caller left his or her finger on the bell-push so that it rang without a break.

The door was opened by Joyce and Dorothy Bray from number 23, ran in and blurted out that she had just shot her husband. Edward Hockless wasted no time in calling for the police and medical assistance. Soon afterwards, Dorothy Bray was escorted to the Bitterne police station.

It was at the station that Dorothy explained that her husband, George Malcom Bray, had threatened to kill her and kept her prisoner in her own home. Early that evening he had grabbed her around the throat with both hands but she managed to get away from him and went to her bedroom, hoping that he might calm down. Meanwhile, she could hear him, in the lounge, talking to himself and threatening to hit her when she returned. When she did go back into the lounge, some minutes later, George did indeed grab hold of her again but once more she managed to escape. She went back to her bedroom, took a shotgun she had purchased some months before, and shot George at close range. On her own statement, forty-six-year-old Dorothy was then charged with murder.

Dorothy Bray had actually been born in Sydney, Australia, and had first met her future husband when he was in the merchant navy during the war. They started seeing each other and after romance had blossomed, they married, in October 1942. One son was born to the union but by the time Dorothy had been charged with killing her husband, he was grown up and married himself.

After the war had ended, George had started work in the building trade, first in Australia and then in the United Kingdom. After some time in England, the family returned to Australia but in 1965 they had come back to Britain again and settled in Southampton where George had become a partner in a firm of carpenters. At the end of that same year, the couple had moved into 23 Robere House.

The problem was that George was, in effect, two people, very much a Jekyll and Hyde character. When he was sober he was somewhat morose but had an even enough temper. However, when he was drunk he became violent, argumentative and threatening and, unfortunately, George was extremely fond of a certain brand of cider. When he was in drink, George often struck out at Dorothy and she had left him on more than one occasion, always returning when he told her he would change his ways. Things did not improve, though, and in September 1966, Dorothy gave a false name and address when she purchased a second-hand 12-bore shotgun and two boxes of cartridges from a second-hand shop in Southampton.

On the day of George's death, he had started drinking his cider in the early afternoon. One bottle after another was consumed and as he drank, his temper grew worse and worse. So bad did things become that, fearful for her own life, Dorothy had taken the only course of action she felt as left open to her.

Nevertheless, she had still taken a life and the law had to run its course.

After various remands by the magistrates, including one on 16 June, one on 23 June and another on 28 June, Dorothy was sent for trial on a charge of murder. She duly appeared before Mister Justice Milmo on 20 July, where she was defended by Mr George Polson. The case for the prosecution was outlined by Mr John Hall. Dorothy pleaded not guilty to murder but guilty to manslaughter. That plea was accepted by the prosecution and further details of the crime were then heard.

Joyce Hockless told the court of Dorothy rushing into her flat on the day of the shooting. She seemed to be very upset and was shaking with fear. Dorothy had blurted out: 'Joyce, I have killed George. I have killed him with a shotgun.' She was distressed and immediately expressed regret for what she had done.

Detective Inspector Arthur Offer had visited the scene of the shooting and searched the premises. He had found five empty quart bottles of cider in the flat. A sixth bottle was partly empty.

Dr Richard Anthony Goodbody had conducted the post-mortem and he described a gunshot wound to George's chest. Only one shot had been fired and the cause of death had been haemorrhage due to that gunshot wound.

The weapon used had been tested, by Dr George Price of the Home Office Laboratory in Nottingham. It had a normal pull and, after testing various distances, Dr Price concluded that the gun had been fired at George Bray from a distance of between three and four feet.

Details of the history of the couple were given to the court. In 1949, whilst they had been living in Australia, George had once tried to throw Dorothy over the verandah of their house on to some rocks twenty feet below, during an argument. He had seriously assaulted her in September 1966 and it was this event which had led to Dorothy purchasing the shotgun for protection and to frighten her violent husband into leaving her alone. She had told her son of the purchase and whilst it might have led to a suggestion of premeditation, the defence pointed out that the gun had been in the flat for some nine months before Dorothy had felt she had no choice but to use it.

One of the final witnesses was Dr Norman Mullen, the medical officer at Holloway prison where Dorothy had been kept on remand. Dr Mullen had spoken to Dorothy at length and he believed that at the time of the shooting, she had been suffering from an abnormality of the mind, caused by the constant mistreatment at the hands of her husband.

It was perhaps, all of this testimony which led the court to accept that Dorothy Bray had lived in genuine fear of her husband, when he was drunk. As a result, Dorothy was given a sentence of three years imprisonment.

Chapter 11

Easy Money
Kenneth Frank Vincent,
William Warren and
Peter John Daley
1967

ighty-four-year-old Elizabeth Harriett Dymott, a retired teacher, had lived alone in a rather dilapidated bungalow at 37 Onibury Road, Southampton, ever since the death of her sister on Christmas Day 1966. She did have another sister, still alive, but that lady was blind and lived in a residential care home. Something of a recluse, Elizabeth's only

The house at 37 Onibury Road where Elizabeth Dymott was killed.

regular caller was a nephew, Thomas William Dymott. Thomas would call on his aunt on a fairly regular basis to make sure she was well. Her only other visitor was a jobbing gardener, Leonard King, who called occasionally to trim trees or do other odd-jobs about the gardens.

Thomas Dymott had last visited his aunt on Tuesday, 21 November when she appeared to be in good health and showed no signs of being worried or concerned about anything. He next called at Onibury Road two weeks later, on Wednesday, 6 December 1967, at 10.30am. There was no reply to his knocking at the front door so Thomas walked around to the back, only to find that the door was partly open. Going inside he switched on a light to find obvious signs that the place had been ransacked; drawers were open, and items were strewn around the floor. In addition, the gas-meter had been broken open. Thomas began walking from room to room until finally,

The rear of the house, in Onibury Road, showing the window which had been forced open.

Inside Elizabeth Dymott's bedroom showing the signs of disarray after the attackers had searched the premises looking for cash. Note the wrought iron bedstead to which Elizabeth had been tied.

in the bedroom, he found Elizabeth tied to her own bed. She was clearly dead and Thomas dashed next door to use the telephone to call for the police.

The first police officer on the scene was Constable Geoffrey Draper who timed his arrival at 10.40am. He made a quick examination of the premises, including the bedroom where Elizabeth lay, but touched nothing, and waited for other officers to arrive. Detective Inspector Arthur Offer arrived just five minutes later, at 10.45am. He noted that Elizabeth's hands were tied together and then tied to the head of the bed itself. The poor woman had also been gagged, no doubt so that she could not shout for help.

In fact, the body could have been found much earlier than it actually was. Elizabeth was well known for never leaving her front gate open. If a delivery man or the postman ever left it open, she would immediately rush out and close it. On the morning of 28 November, the gate had been left open by the postman and remained that way until Elizabeth's body was found. The neighbours, it seemed, had shown little interest in Elizabeth's welfare.

The living room at 37 Onibury Road, again showing signs that someone had searched the premises.

Later that same day, 6 December, Detective Constable Francis Perry and Detective Sergeant Crossland both arrived at Onibury Road. They made a careful search of the house and noted that someone had forced an entry through the living room window at the back of the premises. There were marks, made by some kind of instrument, on the window and, when this area was examined, by Mr Allen Hill of the fingerprint department, a diamond shaped pattern was seen. Similar marks were later found on one of the bedroom doors inside the house. Other, unidentified prints were found inside the house and this led officers to consider a mass fingerprinting of the area, as a last resort. In the event, some 1,500 sets were taken, but they did not move the investigation forward in any way.

Amongst the property found inside the house, was an old silver threepenny piece, dated 1889, which had a hole in it as if it might once have been fastened onto a charm bracelet. There was also a good deal of money hidden in various locations and in all, officers eventually found thirty-three £10 notes, three £5 notes, six hundred and sixteen £1 notes and twenty ten-shilling notes. There was also a small quantity of silver and copper. Whoever had broken into the house had missed over £1,000 in cash.

Dr Yetman was called to the scene at 11.00am. He saw that the hands showed a great deal of bruising, due to the binding around them being so tight. He was also able to say that it appeared that Elizabeth might have been dead for some considerable time.

A check with the neighbours confirmed that Elizabeth kept herself to herself. She had been an independent woman but, at the request of her relatives, neighbours had kept an eye open for her. She had actually last been seen alive, returning from the shops, on 27 November. That was the day Elizabeth had last collected her pension and it was her habit to then do her shopping for the week. This meant that at this stage, the attack upon her could have taken place at any time between that date, and the day her body was discovered, 6 December. House to house enquiries were set in place around a one and a half mile radius, with officers asking if anyone had seen anything suspicious between those two dates.

By now a full post-mortem had been carried out by Dr Arthur Keith Mant, a pathologist from Guy's Hospital. He had first seen Elizabeth's body on the afternoon of 6 December, in situ. He noted that her legs were hanging over the edge of the bed. Pin-point haemorrhages, were seen in the eyes; a sure sign of strangulation or asphyxia. A thin cord had been circled three times around Elizabeth's left wrist and twice around her right, and then tied to the bed-head. Both hands were now swollen and the left one was badly bruised. In addition, Elizabeth's wrists were badly chaffed where she had struggled against her bonds.

There were actually two gags around her mouth. The inner one was a woollen scarf, which had been knotted. The knot produced was inside Elizabeth's mouth and the ends had been tied quite loosely around her head. The outer gag was a linen slip, which had also been knotted and that knot too had been placed in Elizabeth's mouth. The slip had then been looped twice around her lower face and secured on the right side of her head.

The two gags had forced Elizabeth's tongue towards the back of her throat causing a severe restriction of her airway, though she could still have breathed through her nose. Death had been caused by asphyxiation and hypothermia and Dr Mant felt that Elizabeth must have lived for several hours at least, after being tied up. Prior to her death, she appeared to have been quite physically fit for her age. As for the bruising, that had not been caused by any act of physical violence. Rather the bonds had been so tight that they had restricted the flow of blood.

For a time, the investigation stalled. There were no fingerprints that could be identified, no witnesses and no clues as to who had attacked Elizabeth Dymott. Further, though neighbours had told them of an odd-job man who sometimes called at Elizabeth's property, they had not known his name. In fact, it was not until February of the following year that two men; Alfred Bowers and Noah Ernest Page, came forward to tell officers that Leonard King, was the odd-job man who had worked for Elizabeth. Further, he had told them, back in July 1967, about an old woman he did some work for who didn't trust banks and kept her money in her house in Onibury Road, and she might well be worth robbing.

When he was interviewed, King, a general dealer of 13 St John's Road, Hedge End, confirmed that he had done odd jobs for Elizabeth Dymott, and had started work for her in the summer of 1966, whilst her sister was still alive. He went on to say that in November 1967, he had been to Parkstone to see his father. At the time, his uncle, William Warren, was there. They had chatted a little about the various jobs King was doing and at one stage he mentioned that he was doing some work for an old lady who kept lots of money in her house. One night, soon after this, over a weekend, Warren had called at King's home. There were two other men with him; one was named Sergeant and the other he only knew as 'glasses'. His uncle was driving a van and together the four men drove to Onibury Road where King pointed out number 37. King was then driven back to his home. Finally, King was able to say that one of the men in the van had said something about 'seeing him right' when they next met up, if they 'did the job'.

It was important to pin down the exact date of this visit to King's home. Luckily, on the drive to Onibury Road, 'Glasses' had had a portable radio with him, tuned in to the police channel and King remembered hearing some report about a little boy being missing from home. The police checked their records and found that the report King referred to had been made by Constable Eric William Perriment of the Winchester police. A Mr Gray had made a 999 call to the police reporting that his eight year old son, Kevin, was missing. Constable Perriment had then transmitted the details through to police car 208 at 18.53 on Saturday, November 25th.

It was a simple matter now to trace the men King had referred to. The first of these, Michael Anthony Sergeant, a landscape gardener living at 20 Bryanstone Road in Bournemouth, was also able to say that the van they had used to make the visit in late November 1967 had belonged to him. He had been accompanied by William Warren and Kenneth Vincent. King had told them that the old woman in Onibury Road didn't trust banks and kept her money hidden inside her house. Though King had never been inside the house he had seen that the woman always paid him in £1 notes which she took from a drawer in the kitchen.

Sergeant confirmed King's story of being taken back home after he had shown them which house the old lady lived at. The other three men; Sergeant, Warren and Vincent, had then driven back to the Onibury Road area. They parked the van about half a mile away and went for a walk. At one stage, Sergeant became separated from the other two and by the time he got back to his van, he found that Warren and Vincent were already sitting in the back, waiting for him. Sergeant didn't feel like driving around to drop the others off, so he loaned the van to Vincent who took Sergeant to the top of Bryanstone Road. By arrangement, Sergeant walked to Vincent's house the following morning, at 8.30am, to pick the van up.

As far as the police were concerned this testimony seemed to suggest that Warren and Vincent had shown a rather keen interest in the house where Elizabeth Dymott lived in Onibury Road. The attack upon her could not, however, have taken place the same night since Elizabeth had been seen alive two days later, on Monday, 27 November. It was time to interview Warren and Vincent.

When he was interviewed, William Warren confirmed that he had first heard of the old woman who had money hidden in her house, from his nephew, 'Lenny' in November 1967. A week or so later Warren, together with Vincent and 'Sango' (Sergeant) had driven to King's house and he had then come with them to show them the exact house where Elizabeth lived. He also confirmed that King had been dropped off at home and, after this night, Sango had taken no further part in events.

Over the next few days, Kenneth Vincent and a third man, Peter Daley, had visited Warren two or three times and tried to persuade him to join with them in robbing the woman from Onibury Road. He didn't want to get involved, as the house was occupied by a very old lady.

Then, one night, Daley and Vincent drove over again in two separate vehicles. Daley was driving a yellow Hillman car whilst Vincent had a blue Morris van. All three men climbed into the van and Vincent again suggested that they rob Elizabeth, as it would be easy money. Warren was hoping to find some metal to sell but the other two seemed much more interested in ready cash. Once again, they drove to Onibury Road where they arrived at around 7.00pm.

Vincent was driving the van and he parked behind some flats. The three men then all walked towards the back of Elizabeth's house where Daley prised open a window with a chisel. Daley then went inside only to return a few minutes later to say that the woman who lived there was in bed. At that point, Daley and Vincent pulled silk stockings over their heads and Daley took some rope out of his pocket, saying that he intended tying the woman up. Warren wanted nothing to do with this and walked back to where the van was parked.

According to Warren's story he then sat in the van for some two hours before the other two returned. At one stage he had paced up and down outside the van and asked a man who was passing if he had a light for his cigarette. That man was aged about fifty, some five feet seven inches tall, wearing a dark jacket and trousers and a white shirt. He had a small white spaniel or terrier with him.

In due course, Vincent and Daley returned. Vincent was still wearing some rubber gloves and Warren said that they might have been yellow but he wasn't sure on that point. The two men confirmed that they had tied Elizabeth up and said that they had taken somewhere between £150 and £200. They also had some shillings and two gold sovereigns. Warren told the others that it would be a good idea for them to telephone the police and tell them, anonymously, that an old lady was tied up in her house but Daley was worried that the police might trace the call and argued against the idea. Warren said that he would go to the police station if Daley didn't make the telephone call. At the time they had stopped the van by the White Hart public house at Ringwood, where there was a public call box. Reluctantly, Daley then walked across to the box, returned after a minute or so, and said he had made the call.

The three men then drove to Vincent's house where they had a cup of tea. Daley then shared out the money they had taken and one third of it was handed over to Warren. He, however, did not want his share and said that later he had burnt it. Less than two weeks later, there was a report on the television that Elizabeth Dymott had been found dead in her house. That same night, Vincent came to Warren's house and told him not to say a word to anyone. He pointed out that Warren was involved as was Leonard King and if it came out, they'd both probably get ten years in jail.

Peter Daley's statement was somewhat different. He said that he had been talked into his involvement in the crime. It had been Warren who told him that they would have to tie up the old woman and he hadn't really wanted to do that. Possibly to make him feel better about things, Warren had said that the money was in a desk just inside the back door and if they went in that way, they might not even see the woman who lived there.

On the night of the crime, all three men had gone inside the house; Warren, Vincent and Daley himself. They searched the kitchen but didn't find much so decided to go into the bedroom. Elizabeth was asleep but woke up when they entered and tried to grab the man nearest to her, which happened to be Daley. Someone, he wasn't sure who, had then grabbed Elizabeth's hands and tried to stop her from shouting for help. Vincent produced a rope and tied Elizabeth's hands.

Elizabeth asked the men what they wanted and when they said they were after her money, she offered to show them where it was but as soon as they let her get up, she started shouting. Someone covered her mouth with some material and Warren went to the back door to see if anyone had heard Elizabeth's shouts.

An envelope was discovered on a chair at the foot of the bed and this contained a good deal of banknotes. The men also found a jewellery box, which also contained some money. At this point Vincent complained that it was hurting his arms to keep hold of Elizabeth and said it would be better to tie her up. Vincent tied her hands to the bedstead whilst Warren held Elizabeth still.

The men then searched the house and at one stage Vincent noticed the gas meter in the kitchen. He broke this open and took the shilling coins from inside it. By this time Warren was outside, standing a few yards from the house and mentioned that he might have been seen by a neighbour. It was time to leave. Warren was driving and he refused to stop at the call box so that Daley could telephone the police. He was eventually persuaded that they didn't need to call the authorities as it surely wouldn't be long before someone found Elizabeth and untied her.

Kenneth Vincent did not make a formal statement. He merely told Detective Constable John Jones: 'I didn't intend this to happen to her. It has gone wrong.' Later he added: 'You may not believe this but when I saw what had happened to her on the television, I nearly went and gave myself up. I was going to say I was the only chap on the job. Do you believe that?' Later still, Vincent spoke to Detective Inspector Graham Swain and said that when this all came to court he intended to plead guilty adding: 'The books are stacked against me. I will defend myself.'

In the event, all three men were charged with murder. Various remands followed and the evidence was finally laid before the magistrates on 2 May 1968. In fact, one further adjournment was required and it was not until 10 May that it was decided to send them to the next Hampshire assizes to face their trial. All three men were charged with conspiracy in addition to murder.

The case had attracted a good deal of publicity and public feeling ran high. For this reason an application was made to try the case outside of Hampshire. The hearing on this took place on 21 May when it was stated that Warren had sought publicity, which might prove detrimental to the other two defendants. As a result, the trial of all three men was transferred to London.

The trial of Warren, Daley and Vincent opened on 9 July 1968, before Mister Justice Waller at the Old Bailey with Mr John Wilmers appearing for the prosecution.

Despite his earlier statements, Vincent, like the other two, pleaded not guilty to murder, but guilty to conspiracy to steal, and was defended by Mr John Stocker.

Detective Constable Perry told the court of the diamond shaped patterns he had found at the scene of the crime. On 7 March 1968, he had gone to Vincent's house at 17 Teddar Road, Bournemouth and searched the premises. He had found a pair of rubber gloves with a moulded diamond pattern, and these matched the marks found at Elizabeth's house. He had also found an 1889 sixpence with a hole bored through it. It should be remembered that a threepence piece, also dated 1889 and with a hole in it, had been found at the house. The holes in the two coins were checked for size and position and it was found that they corresponded exactly.

Detective Constable Frederick Meader told the court that he had visited the murder scene at 3.00pm on the afternoon of 6 December, when he helped other officers make a search of the house. He had found two letters on the doormat and these were postmarked 27 November and 1 December, respectively. The postman for this address, Alfred James Boyce, told the court that he believed he had delivered a letter to Elizabeth's address on 28 November.

In addition to the two letters, a church magazine had been found, stuffed into the letterbox but not pushed all the way through. Dorothy Irene Young testified that she had delivered

The two letters found on the mat inside Elizabeth Dymott's house. These enabled officers to pinpoint the most probable date of the attack.

that magazine on 4 December. All this testimony implied that the attack upon Elizabeth had most probably taken place on the evening of Monday, 27 November, the date she had last been seen alive by a neighbour, as she was returning from the shops.

Detective Constable Leslie Reginald Newman had examined the gas meter at the premises. The lock had been forced and the coin container was empty. That gas meter had last been read by Albert Edward Beeson, a collection officer for the Southern Gas Board. He testified that on 3 October, the figures read 4985.

Albert Frank Butler was a special meter collector and from the present reading of 5004, he calculated that the collection box should have contained £1 6s in shilling coins.

Medical evidence was given by Dr Arthur Mant who had examined Elizabeth's body at her home, and later performed the post-mortem. He testified that she had had a zero chance of survival once she was left tied up. The cords used to bind her were so strong that even a fit, strong person would have been unable to escape from them. Indeed, once the body had been found, the bonds had to be cut off by the police.

On 16 July, Vincent stepped into the witness box to tell his story. As he was being shown police pictures of the body of Elizabeth Dymott, Warren sobbed in court and shouted: 'Dirty Dogs.'

The following day, 17 July, Lillian Warren, the wife of William, testified that at the magistrate's court hearings, one of the other two, Vincent, had told her that her husband had taken no part in the crime. His exact words were: 'No, Bill was not in the house.'

On 18 July, the jury of ten men and two women retired at 12.35pm. They had been told that there were three possible verdicts on the murder charge; guilty, not guilty of murder but guilty of manslaughter and finally, not guilty. In the event, the verdicts, when they came, were that Daley and Warren were guilty of manslaughter, and two other offences. Vincent was judged to be not guilty but since he had earlier pleaded guilty to conspiracy to steal, he too would face a prison sentence.

In the event, Daley and Warren were both sentenced to twenty years for manslaughter, twelve years for robbery and six years for conspiracy, all the sentences to be served concurrently. Vincent received six years for the conspiracy charge.

An appeal against those sentences was entered and heard on Monday, 3 February 1969 before Lord Justice Winn, Lord Justice Widgery and Mister Justice Lawton. They held that whilst the crime had been a dreadful act, the sentences had, nevertheless, been too severe. The sentences on Warren and Daley were reduced from twenty years to fifteen, whilst Vincent's six years' was reduced to four.

Chapter 12

The Brothers John Henry De Lara and Owen William De Lara 1969

olice Constable Frederick James Tyler, a member of the harbour police, was on duty in the Town Quay office during the early hours of Monday, 28 July 1969, when he heard the protesting sound of a car ignition being turned.

Glancing at his watch, Tyler saw that it was 3.00am and as he stepped outside of the station he heard the ignition again. Looking up the road he saw that there was a car backing out of Bugle Street into Western Esplanade. The vehicle was facing him now, with its headlights on and even as he watched, Tyler heard the starter motor another three or four times. The officer climbed into his own car and drove down to investigate.

As he approached, Tyler saw that the vehicle in question was a dark coloured Ford Anglia estate car, registration 341 KHO and there were two men inside; one in the driver's seat and one in the front passenger seat. Tyler asked them what the problem was and the driver replied that he thought he was out of petrol.

Constable Tyler wanted to know more and asked the driver for his name. He said he was John Edison but gave no reply when asked for the vehicle's registration number. Satisfied that something wasn't quite right here, Tyler then turned to the passenger who said he was John's brother. Neither man could produce any documents or identification so Tyler demanded that they accompany him back to the station. The Ford was secured and both men then climbed into Constable Tyler's car. There, Tyler told the men that he was not satisfied with their explanation, believed that the vehicle they were driving might

The company car used by Kenneth Giles and stolen by John De Lara. The car was also used to dump Giles' body.

well be stolen and said that he was calling for help from the Hampshire Constabulary.

The two men were escorted back to the Town Quay police office from where Constable Tyler did indeed ring for assistance. It wasn't very long before Constable Alfred Edmunds arrived and, after some questioning by both Tyler and Edmunds, the two men finally gave their correct names. The driver of the car identified himself as John Henry De Lara and his passenger was indeed his brother, Owen William De Lara. They were then asked who the car they had been driving actually belonged to and John said that he had seen it outside the *Horse and Groom* pub in East Street, with the keys in the ignition, and had simply taken it. They were then told that they would be taken to the Civic Centre police station whereupon, within the space of a few minutes, both of the De Laras asked to use the toilet.

At 3.30am, Constable Geoffrey William Flowers arrived at the Town Quay station and assisted Constable Edmunds to take the prisoners to the Civic Centre. Before they left, Flowers was given a pair of gloves, which John had said he didn't need anymore and had thrown into a bin. It was believed that these gloves might be evidence in any case that might develop.

The Civic Centre. It was here that the De Lara brothers were interviewed and later charged.

It was also before the De Laras were taken in that two searches were organised. Constables Flowers and Tyler first searched the Ford Anglia. They found a wallet underneath the driver's seat which contained two £5 notes and two £1 notes. Then the two officers searched the toilet which the two brothers had both used. In the cistern they discovered a gold watch and a man's ring.

By 4.30am, both prisoners were in the parade room at the Civic Centre police station. Detective Constable Edward David Roberts was given all the details thus far, and received the items which Constable Edmunds had brought with him. By now, both men had been searched and amongst the items found on them was a bunch of keys, a Dunhill lighter, and an empty cigarette case. These, along with the wallet, pair of gloves, the watch and ring, were all entered into evidence.

A further interview took place and John De Lara admitted that he had taken the car at around 11.30pm. Outlining his movements of the previous evening he said he had been to a few public houses including the *Beehive* and the *Nags Head*. He had not actually gone inside the *Horse and Groom* but had seen the car outside and taken it. He had then gone to pick up his brother Owen, by which time it was midnight or perhaps even 12.30am, and they had driven around the city. At first, he denied knowing anything about the watch and the ring found in the cistern at the police station but eventually admitted he had left them there, claiming that he had found them in the car.

Still the questioning continued and Constable Roberts explained that he was concerned about the owner of the car. The officers did not believe that John had found the car with the keys in the ignition and felt that he might have attacked the owner in order to steal his car. Then, suddenly, John altered the entire line of the investigation by announcing: 'He's dead.'

John went on to make a full statement part of which read: 'I was in the *Horse and Groom*. I was only drinking small browns like. I went to the toilet and I saw two queers in the bar.'

'At half-ten I walked down the road towards Edwin Jones [a local shop] when he picked me up in his car and asked me if I wanted a lift. He took me home and I asked him in for a cup of coffee. While I was in the kitchen he came in and touched me up. Something went click and I went berserk.'

The kitchen at 92, Wimpson Lane, Millbrook, where Kenneth Giles was attacked and killed by John De Lara.

John went on to say that he had torn the electric flex from an iron, and used it to strangle his victim. He had then dumped the body somewhere in the New Forest, on a side road close to Lymington.

Once all these details had been taken down in writing, John was placed into a police car with Detective Constable Roberts and Detective Constable Ballard in an attempt to find the location of the body dump. Somewhere along the A35, between Totton and Ashurst, John said he thought they had gone left up ahead and recalled driving past a pub named the *Swan*. This establishment was just past Lyndhurst but, despite the best efforts of the two officers, no trace of the car owner could be found.

By now, the keeper of the stolen vehicle had been identified. Kenneth John Giles lived at 5 Ascupart House, Bevois Valley, Southampton with his common law wife, Caroline Margaret. Though the couple were not actually married, Caroline had changed her name, by deed poll, and she had lived as Kenneth's wife for some fourteen years.

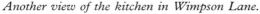

Another view of the kitchen in Wimpson Lane.

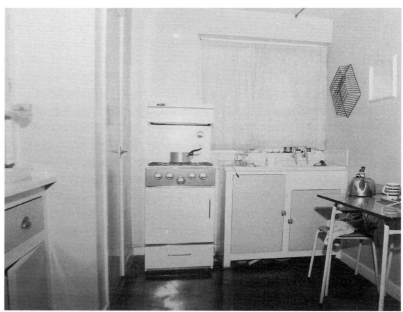

When Caroline was interviewed she told the police that Kenneth had been born on 19 August 1912, at Exmouth. He worked as a shipping manager for Wilmot Packaging and the car in question had been a company car. Caroline went on to say that she knew that Kenneth had homosexual tendencies and at one stage, she had left him for a period of eighteen months because of this. She also stated that, despite being together for so long, she had never had sexual intercourse with him. Turning to the night in question, Sunday, 27 July, Caroline said that Kenneth had left home at around 7.00pm to go to the *Highfield* pub. He had the company car with him at the time and she would have expected him to return no later than midnight.

The use of the car was confirmed by Wilfrid Sandiford, the works manager for Wilmot's of Salisbury Road, Totton. He confirmed that Kenneth Giles had worked for the company since 30 August 1962. Part of his duties involved a good deal of travel and he had been allowed to use various company cars for this purpose. Since the summer of 1967, the car allocated to him was a blue Ford Anglia registration 341 KHO and Kenneth had had exclusive use of that vehicle since 14 May 1969.

At this stage, John De Lara had admitted that he strangled Kenneth Giles and then dumped his body but what had the involvement been of Owen, his brother? Officers began speaking to John's neighbours at Wimpson Lane, Millbrook. Leslie Colin Dear lived in flat 86 with his mother and their sitting room was directly underneath John De Lara's flat at 92. Leslie reported that at around 11.00pm on 27 July, he had heard a loud noise, coming from the flat above. It sounded like furniture being thrown onto the floor and Leslie assumed that John had come home drunk and knocked something over.

Frank James Cousins lived at flat 90 and some half an hour after the noise had been heard by Leslie Dear, Frank was heading to bed when he drew back the curtains in his lounge. Looking down into the street he saw a blue Ford parked on the footpath. The following morning, the car had gone.

Of more import perhaps, was the testimony of Lilian Gorton who lived in flat 84. She had retired for the night at some time between 10.30pm and 11.00pm on 27 July but after some time she was woken by a noise outside her window. Lilian got out of bed and looked outside. She saw three men leaving the flats together, but one of them was being carried by the other two. She assumed that he was drunk and the others were helping him home. She recognised one of the men as the man who lived at number 92, John De Lara and at one stage, one of the men said: 'Don't drop it now. Don't drop it now.' From this evidence, it appeared that Owen had taken an active part in the disposal of Kenneth's body.

To check on this, officers spoke to Patricia Joyce De Lara, Owen's wife at their home, 14 Oslo Towers, Weston, South-ampton. She explained that she and Owen had been married for four and a half years but had no children yet. Indeed, Owen was due to take some medical advice soon, on the possibility of having a family.

Referring to the weekend she told officers that her husband's birthday was 24 July whilst her brother's was 25 July. For that reason, they had spent the weekend at her brother Walter's house but had returned to Oslo Towers at around 11.30pm on 27 July. They had had something to eat and were watching television when there was a knock on the front door. Owen went out to answer it and Patricia could hear raised voices in the hallway. She went out to see who had called at this time of night to find John, who looked extremely upset.

Patricia asked John what the matter was and was shocked to hear him say that he had just '. . . strangled a bloke'. He pleaded with Owen to help him get rid of the body and Owen, quite correctly, said that he would go to the police with John and explain what had happened. John would have none of it and said: 'No, I'll get life.' Patricia made some coffee and, after some discussion, Owen agreed to help and the two brothers left the house together in the early hours of 28 July.

Meanwhile, the search for the missing man's body continued. By speaking to both John and Owen, the police were able to narrow down the area they were referring to. The area around Lyndhurst was visited again and eventually the two brothers spotted a grass verge they recognised. At one stage, John had reversed onto the verge, which was at the edge of a driveway and it was here, in Ornamental Drive, Bolderwood, that officers

The lane leading to the spot where Kenneth Giles' body was finally discovered. Notice the police officer guarding the location.

finally found the bracken-covered body of Kenneth Giles. John De Lara was now charged with murder and his brother Owen with assisting an offender.

The trial of the two men opened on Tuesday, 2 December 1969, before Mister Justice Fisher and a jury of nine men and three women. The case for the prosecution was outlined by Mr Peter H R Bristow, assisted by Mr Robert Hughes, whilst John was defended, on the murder charge, by Mr Ian Starforth Hill and Mr Richard Bain. Owen was defended by Mr Raymond Stock and Mr David Owen Thompson.

After the various police witnesses had been heard, Caroline Giles repeated her story of Kenneth having left home on the night of 27 July. The following evening she had been taken to the mortuary where she made a formal identification of the body. She had also identified various items as ones belonging to Kenneth. These included the watch and ring recovered from the cistern in the police station toilet and the wallet found on John De Lara.

The body of Kenneth Giles in situ. Only bracken covering the body has been removed.

June Stewart was a part-time barmaid in the *Horse and Groom* public house, and had been for the past fifteen years. She knew all of the regular customers quite well and was behind the bar on 27 July from 7.00pm until around 10.30pm. At some time between 9.00pm and 9.30pm, a customer she knew as John had come into the bar. He had sat in his usual seat and chatted for a time with Dennis Jones, one of the barmen. June had known John for some time and also was aware that he was a homosexual. John, of course, was Kenneth John Giles, who had apparently preferred to use his second name when frequenting public houses around the city.

Confirmation could be given of the approximate time that Kenneth's body had been dumped in Ornamental Drive. Bertie Benjamin Smith was a head keeper in the New Forest and lived in a cottage at the top of a long driveway. On the night of 27 July, he had gone to bed at midnight. He slept soundly but was woken by the sound of a car engine being revved very hard, in his driveway. He glanced at his watch and saw that it was some time after 2.00am. The noise died down and Bertie went back to sleep. The following morning he found vehicle tracks on the grass verge which separated his cottage from the main road.

The initial medical examination and the subsequent post-mortem had been carried out by Dr Peter Pullar. He reported marks of a double ligature around the neck of the dead man indicating that a thin material had been wound around the throat twice before being tightened. An object such as the electric flex collected by the police, could have made those wounds. Dr Pullar confirmed that the cause of death was strangulation by means of a ligature.

Carole Ann De Lara was John's estranged wife and now lived at 9 Redbridge Towers, Millbrook. She told the court that she and John had married on 20 December 1965 at which time, John was in the army. The couple had two children: Anthony who was now three and Amanda Jane who was eighteen months. John, however, was not the father of the youngest child.

Carole went on to explain that on 31 May 1967, at Munster in Germany, John had been sentenced to one year's imprisonment by an army court martial for assault occasioning actual bodily harm and malicious damage. With another soldier he had broken into the Other Ranks Club and damaged beyond repair a juke box, two games machines and some bar furniture. As for the assault charges, apparently John had goaded a much smaller man in his unit, sometimes rousing him from his sleep and forcing him to engage in boxing practice against his will.

Whilst John was serving his sentence in Germany and just before he was due to be released, Carole had found the flat at 92 Wimpson Lane and had moved in there on 10 January 1968. John had returned home and joined his family ten days later, on 20 January. Immediately he had obtained work as a labourer at Montague Meyer Limited but that job didn't last very long, John being dismissed soon afterwards. He then found employment as a packer at Dimplex.

There were, however, some marital problems. As Carole had already explained, Amanda was not John's child. She had had a brief relationship whilst he was in prison and, whilst she had been confined to hospital during her daughter's birth, Carole had discovered that John had been entertaining a sixteen-year-old girl at their flat. They had words about this and, in the heat of the argument, John had hit her. Carole had then gone to live with her mother for a short time but soon returned to Wimpson Lane.

The couple argued again in June 1969 during which John banged Carole's head into the larder door two or three times. As a result of this and the continued strained relationship, Carole returned to her mother's house on 5 July and had been there ever since.

In the event, on the second and final day of the trial, after all the prosecution evidence had been heard, Owen De Lara changed his plea to guilty on an amended charge. That charge was now: 'That on July 28th last, at Southampton, after John De Lara had committed an arrestable offence, knowing or believing him to be guilty of the offence or some other arrestable offence, without lawful authority or excuse, assisted John De Lara to take the body of Kenneth John Giles from 92 Wimpson Lane and to conceal the same at Bolderwood, near Lyndhurst, with intent to impede the apprehension or prosecution of John De Lara.' For that offence, Owen would eventually receive a sentence of eighteen months' imprisonment, suspended for two years.

As for John De Lara, after an absence of four hours, the jury could only return a majority verdict. Eleven members of the jury agreed that he was guilty of murder whilst one dissented. As a result, John was sentenced to life imprisonment with a recommendation that he serve a minimum of ten years. He appealed against that sentence almost a year later, on 12 November 1970, but his plea was dismissed and the sentence was confirmed.

Chapter 13

History Repeating Itself
Stephen Michael Marley
1973

On October 1947, the Union Castle ship *Durban Castle* left Capetown in South Africa, bound for Southampton. Somewhere along the journey, James Camb disposed of the body of Gay Gibson, only to find himself charged with her murder. Then, in September 1973, another ship, the *Rotherwick Castle*, another vessel of the Union Castle line, also left Capetown, bound for Southampton and once again, one of the passengers would never get to complete her journey, and another man would face a charge of murder.

There was in fact one big difference between the ships in these two stories. The *Durban Castle* had been a passenger ship

The Rotherwick Castle *on which Michelle Kirkwood met her death at the hands of Stephen Marley.*

but the *Rotherwick Castle* was a cargo ship and as such, she was not entitled to take passengers. This, however, did not deter two young friends; Michelle Kirkwood and Linda Von-Waltzleben, who decided to become stowaways in South Africa.

The ship was docked at Capetown from 1–4 September 1973. During that time there was a small party thrown by the crew and four South African girls were invited on board to join the festivities. Two of these girls were Michelle and Linda, both of whom earned their living as prostitutes, their 'pitch' being the waterfront. The two girls had been on the ship a few times before whilst it was in port, but this time they decided that they didn't want to leave. So it was that when the *Rotherwick Castle* left port on 4 September, Michelle and Linda hid themselves in the cabin of one of the crew; Stephen Michael Marley.

On 21 September, the ship docked in Southampton. Marley, and another member of the crew, Anthony Turner, then smuggled Linda off the ship and out of the dockyard, after which she was given a lift to Basingstoke railway station. As for Michelle Kirkwood, she was nowhere to be seen, for she had never completed the journey to England.

On the day after the *Rotherwick Castle* had docked, 22 September, Linda Von-Waltzleben made her mind up to hitch-hike to Herne Bay, where Stephen Marley lived. She was fortunate in quickly obtaining a lift from James Francis Gaitens, a consultant biologist who lived in Sittingbourne. He agreed to take Linda as far as his home town and dropped her off at the railway station that afternoon, after first giving her his contact details in case she needed further help. Later, Linda telephoned Mr Gaitens, saying she had got lost, and as a result he picked her up, took her to his house, introduced her to his wife, and all three then had dinner together. It was during that meal that Linda told him that Marley had dumped Michelle's body over the side of the ship.

Mr Gaitens couldn't simply take this story at face value and decided that further enquiries were needed. He telephoned Marley's home, where he lived with his parents, and asked the family to come over to his house, telling them that an accusation had been made against Stephen. Some forty-five minutes later, the Marleys arrived and Mr Gaitens took them to an empty

A closer view of the Rotherwick Castle, *showing where Michelle's body was dumped overboard.*

room, away from Linda, and asked Stephen directly what had happened on the ship. Marley freely admitted throwing a girl overboard. It was all they needed to hear and Marley's father immediately contacted the police.

At this stage, there was no question of a murder charge. No report of such a crime had been made and no body had been found. Marley was escorted to the police station where he was interviewed by CID officers from both Kent and Hampshire. He was cautioned and after questioning admitted that he had put the girl overboard after squeezing her neck because she was drunk and screaming and had broken a model boat that he had been making. He went on to say that he was also drunk at the time. Meanwhile, Linda Von-Waltzleben had also been detained, as an illegal immigrant.

In fact, Linda might well have faced other charges. After she had told her story to the police, there was evidence that she had assisted an offender but it was felt that prosecuting her for that might have jeopardised the chance of building a strong enough case against Marley. For that reason, the Hampshire police, who were in charge of the case, decided not to take the matter further, as far as Linda was concerned.

On Sunday 23 September, Detective Chief Inspector Moyce and Detective Inspector Arthur Offer escorted Marley back to Southampton and the Civic Centre police station. The prisoner was formally interviewed the following day, in the presence of his solicitor, Mr Yeo and on Tuesday, 25 September, Marley made his first appearance before the magistrates in Southampton, when he was remanded in custody whilst further evidence was collected.

Other people had been mentioned by Linda when she had told her story and these individuals were now interviewed by the police.

Anthony Turner was another of the crew members on board the *Rotherwick Castle* and he confirmed that he had seen both girls at the party before the ship left South Africa. He did not know they had remained on board when the ship left port until he found them both in an empty cabin, which was opposite to Marley's. He reported his find to Marley who said that they could both stay in his cabin as they would be less likely to be seen.

Turner also said that he had taken food to the girls but knew nothing about a party which was alleged to have taken place on 15 September, though he did visit the cabin during the afternoon and had a double whisky and coca-cola. He did not stay long and whilst he was there, Michelle did drink some of the whisky. Whilst Turner was in the cabin, Marley had left to go and play football with some other members of the crew. Turner himself left after a few minutes and next went to the cabin at around 8.00pm, in order to borrow a radio from Marley. Turner had to knock on the door no less than seven times before Marley opened it and when he did so, Turner saw Linda, who used the nickname 'Fanta', sitting on the end of the bunk. Michelle lay on the bunk, on her back, with her left arm and left leg hanging over the side. There was a black cord or wire around her neck and she had white froth around her mouth. Marley then confessed that he had killed Michelle because they had argued. She had said that she was going to report him for helping her to stowaway once they had reached England and also, during their argument, she had broken a boat he was making, and which he intended to give to his parents as a present.

Once again, the Hampshire police decided that it would be counterproductive to charge Turner with any offence since his testimony against Marley would be more important than any prosecution against him.

William Lowes was a greaser on board the *Rotherwick Castle* and he told officers that he had seen Michelle at the party on board the ship at Capetown. On 16 September, he had seen Linda Von-Waltzleben coming out of Marley's cabin. He spoke to her and he and Linda then went back into the cabin. As they were talking, he saw a comic in the waste-paper bin and picked it up. Blood dripped from the comic and Linda told him that it was Marley's blood. She went on to say that they had argued and she had hit him on the nose, which had then bled. Lowes saw Marley soon afterwards and told him that he had seen Linda. Marley asked him not to say anything to anyone about her being on board. He repeated the plea the following day, 17 September.

Stephen Robert Edward Lingwood was another crew member and he too had seen the girls at the party before the ship left port. Lingwood worked in the ship's mess and once they had sailed, Marley approached him and asked him to put some extra food aside for him. Five days into the voyage to Southampton, Lingwood discovered the reason for this extra food when he found out about the two girls in Marley's cabin. When he mentioned this to Marley, he told Lingwood that them being aboard was Anthony Turner's idea.

Lingwood asked Marley how he intended getting the girls ashore once the ship docked, pointing out that he might have a few problems. Marley, rather strangely perhaps, said that he would rather kill them than have them discovered. Later in the voyage, Linda had told Lingwood that Marley had killed Michelle. The only action Lingwood took on hearing this was to make sure that he stayed out of Marley's way for the rest of the trip. Once again, the police had decided not to take any action against Lingwood, preferring to have him as a witness for the prosecution.

Details of Marley's arrest and Michelle's death were published in various newspapers and one of these reports was seen by Mr Douglas Palomo, who then went to the police station at Beccles. He told officers that he knew Michelle, having first met her in July 1973 when his ship, the *Windsor Castle*, yet another vessel of the Union Castle line, had docked in Capetown. They had become rather friendly and Michelle had asked him a number of times if he would take her to England. These repeated requests caused them to argue and in temper, he tore up a photograph of Michelle, which she had given to him. He had, however, kept the pieces and he now handed these over to the police. The picture was carefully pieced together and when shown to Linda, she immediately confirmed that it was indeed Michelle. The picture was sent to Durban for further confirmation from the South African authorities. In due course, they sent back a positive identification. Michelle Kirkwood was actually Anna Marie Knox and she had been just fifteen years old. Further investigations showed that Linda, alias 'Fanta' was herself just sixteen and had run away from her home in Port Elizabeth some four months earlier.

After various remands before the magistrates, Marley finally faced his trial at Winchester, before Mister Justice Lawson on 29 October 1973. Mr Titheridge and Mr John Bull appeared for the prosecution and Marley pleaded not guilty to the murder of Anna Marie Knox, also known as Michelle Kirkwood.

The first, and most important witness for the prosecution, was Linda Von-Waltzleben. She testified that until 17 May 1973, she

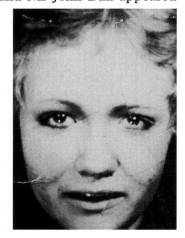

A photograph of Michelle Kirkwood, whose real name was Anna Marie Knox. The marks on the picture show where it was pieced back together, by the police, after Mr Douglas Palomo had torn it up.

had lived with her father and step-mother at Port Elizabeth. She claimed that she had left home because her friends had wanted her to have sexual intercourse with a Chinese man so she went to live with her uncle, George Piper, in Capetown. It was there, whilst visiting the Monte Carlo club, that she had first met the girl she knew as Michelle Kirkwood.

Linda claimed that she had first met the defendant, Marley, in February 1973. They became friends and he told her the name of the ship he worked on. They met again at the Monte Carlo club, once she had moved to her uncle's house, and he told her about a party that was going to take place on the *Rotherwick Castle*. It was at that party that she saw Michelle again and they soon rekindled their friendship. Over the next couple of days, Linda, Michelle and others often visited the nearby *Crazy Horse* public house and it was there, during one of their visits, that they decided to go back to the ship and stow away in order to get to England. They both then went home and packed suitcases before returning to the ship. They stayed in an empty cabin until the ship actually sailed and after this, Michelle initially stayed with one of the crew named Billy Lowes, in his cabin, whilst Linda slept in Marley's cabin, on his couch.

On the third night out, which would be 6 September, Linda and Michelle both stayed in Marley's cabin. Linda slept on the floor whilst Michelle shared the bunk with Marley. Earlier the two girls had argued over boyfriends but they had now made friends again and for the next week or so, the only time either of them left Marley's cabin was when one of them needed to use the toilet.

On about the third or fourth day out from Capetown, Michelle had slashed one of her wrists because she liked Marley but knew they would have to part once the ship reached England. Michelle had used a razor blade to inflict the wound but it was not deep. Linda wrapped a pillowcase around the wound and it stopped bleeding after about twenty minutes. This might well have shown that Michelle was rather highly-strung and subject to mood swings which in turn might explain her later behaviour.

On 15 September, Linda and Michelle were drinking rather heavily and at one stage, Michelle was singing, dancing, and yelling. When Marley tried to restrain her, she kicked out and this caused her to break the model ship, which Marley had been working on. It was her behaviour and the breaking of the model, which caused Michelle and Marley to argue and as words were exchanged, Michelle lay on the bunk. Marley went over to Michelle, pushed her face into the pillow and threatened to kill her if she didn't shut up. Michelle would not be silenced and began to struggle all the more. Then Linda saw him draw something black around Michelle's neck. Linda did not intervene, not only because she was probably too drunk to do so, but also because she thought Marley might attack her too.

After Michelle had fallen still, Marley stuffed her body underneath his bunk and then left the room. He returned some time later and it was clear that Michelle was now dead. Marley asked Linda to help him get rid of the body but she refused. He asked her for a second time and Linda refused again. Marley then left the cabin, carrying Michelle's body with him. He was gone fifteen minutes or so and then returned, alone, saying that he had dumped her over the side of the ship and into the sea.

At 4.00pm on Friday, 21 September, the ship docked at Southampton. Anthony Turner's brother-in-law, William Robert Beedon, had picked up Anthony, Linda and Marley in his car and took them to Basingstoke railway station where Anthony gave her £2 and said he would be back soon. Anthony then drove off with William Beedon whilst Marley accompanied Linda onto the platform. In due course, Marley caught his own train and Linda was left on the station until 11.30pm but Anthony never came back for her. In the meantime, Linda had met a girl named Lynette, who offered to put her up for the night. The next day she decided to travel to Herne Bay which is how she met Mr Gaitens who took her as far as Sittingbourne.

James Gaitens told the court that on 22 September, he had been to Basingstoke with Michael Papp and his wife. These three were all in Mr Gaitens' mini-traveller when they picked up a young girl hitchhiker. Mr and Mrs Papps were dropped off at Godstone and Gaitens then drove Linda to Sittingbourne where he dropped her at the railway station at around 5.30pm, having first purchased a ticket for her, to Herne Bay. He had given Linda his telephone number and told her to call him if she got lost. Linda did indeed ring and James drove over to pick her up again. He then took her to his home at 30 Bourne Grove, Sittingbourne, where his wife made Linda a meal.

During their initial car journey Linda had mumbled something about being a stowaway on a ship, with her friend, and adding that he friend had gone overboard but Mr Gaitens had not taken any real notice of this. Later that night, however, Linda elaborated on her story and mentioned that her friend had been killed and thrown overboard from the ship she had travelled on. She also gave details of Marley's address and telephone number. Mrs Gaitens had then telephoned the Herne Bay police to confirm that a family named Marley did indeed live at the address Linda had mentioned. Mr Gaitens then rang the Marleys and said that 'Fanta' was at his house and that she had said something about being a stowaway and that her friend had been hurt on the ship. The Marleys then agreed to go over to Sittingbourne to sort the matter out. They had duly arrived and when Stephen Marley was asked what had happened he had admitted what he had done but said that only Linda knew anything about it and she wouldn't say anything. It was then that his own father said that he would not be able to live with something like this on his conscience, and should tell the truth. It was Mr Marley who then telephoned for the police.

Anthony Turner confirmed his earlier story. He also reported that after Marley had told him that he had killed Michelle, Turner saw the body with some twin core electric wire tied around her neck. Marley asked him not to report the matter and Turner agreed. The next day, Marley told him that he had thrown Michelle's body overboard.

Keith Martin Jones was another member of the crew on board the ship. He told the court that he had owned an electrical converter, which would power a radio from the ship's electrical supply. He had lent this to Marley and at the time it had a black, two-core wire identical to the one Anthony Turner said he had seen around Michelle's throat.

Marley's own story was then given. At Sittingbourne police station, he had been interviewed by Chief Inspector Berry and admitted that he had been paid off on 21 September but that prior to this he had thrown a girl overboard. During his interview he also admitted that Michelle might well have been alive when he threw her off the ship. Explaining this, Marley said that he had had no intention of killing Michelle and had just wanted to quieten her. After he had attacked her he thought he saw her chest moving up and down, showing that she was still breathing. He stuffed her underneath the bunk so that it wouldn't be seen by anyone coming into his cabin but later, when he went back to check on her, she didn't appear to be breathing anymore and her lips were blue. That was when he decided to throw her overboard. Two days after this, he had put all Michelle's clothes into a suitcase and thrown that overboard as well.

The verdict, when it came, was that Stephen Marley was not guilty of murder but was guilty of manslaughter. Only now could some of the details of Marley's earlier life be given. He had one sister and one brother, both younger than he was. He had just one previous conviction, as a juvenile, for the theft of lead in August 1970, for which he was fined £15. He had had various jobs since leaving school, including being a storeroom boy at Woolworth's and a labourer for a container company. He had joined the Merchant Navy in August 1972.

Although he had escaped the mandatory life sentence for murder, largely because the jury felt that there had been no intention to kill, Marley had still taken the life of a young girl. For that offence, Mr Justice Lawson sentenced Stephen Marley to five years in prison.

Other Executions at Winchester Prison

Those who were executed for murders in and around Southampton all suffered that fate at Winchester prison. There were other executions at this prison between 1868 and the abolition of capital punishment and, for the sake of completeness, details of all these crimes are given here. Where no details are given, the story appears in the main body of this book.

Thomas Smith – 16 November 1874.
Smith was a private in the 20th Hussars and was given punishment drill by Captain Bird at Aldershot on Sunday, 13 September. Smith objected, took his gun and shot Bird dead, later claiming that the shooting had been accidental. Smith was tried at the Old Bailey before Mister Justice Lush.

James Caffyn – 11 February 1878.
Chapter 1 in this volume.

Albert Edward Brown – 31 May 1886.
Chapter 2 in this volume.

James Whelan – 31 May,1886.
A seaman travelling from New York to the River Plate on a British ship, the *Emma J Shore*. Whelan argued with the second mate, George Richardson, who had complained about his work. Threats were then issued by both men, but for several days afterwards, no further trouble occurred.

On Monday, 15 March, the two men argued again and Whelen battered Richardson into semi-consciousness before throwing him overboard. Richardson's body was never recovered. Whelen was sent back to England and sentenced to death by Justice Day. Later, he confessed to two earlier murders

George Clarke – 27 March 1888.
Clarke had been in the army and when he retired, he became the landlord of a public house in Aldershot. Clarke lived with his wife and family, which included a step-daughter, Annie Vaughan. In 1886, when Annie was only sixteen, she had an affair with George, which soon ended. Two years later, on Sunday, 5 February 1888, when she expressed her desire to marry, George said he did not approve and, in a subsequent argument, cut her throat. He was sentenced to death by Mr Justice Field.

Edward Henry Fawcett – 25 August 1891.
Also known as Edward Watts he lived with his wife, in Greenwich but after an argument, she went to live in Portsea with their child. Fawcett followed her on Saturday, 4 April, and when she refused to return with him he shot her four times. Fawcett was the last man executed by James Berry.

George Mason – 6 December 1893.
Also known as George Beckworth, he was a soldier in the East Surrey Regiment, based at Portsdown Hill. On Tuesday, 27 June, he was confined to barracks by Sergeant James Robinson and, in revenge, shot him dead the following day. He was hanged by James Billington.

Samuel Elkins – 18 July 1894.
Shot dead his foreman, William Mitchell in Bournemouth after the latter reported him for dereliction of duty.

Cyrus Knight – 12 December 1894.
A carter who cut his wife's throat after they had argued at their home at Binstead near Alton. Knight had cut his own throat after the crime but prompt medical attention had saved his life.

After he was hanged, however, it was seen that the wound in his neck had opened.

William Rogers – 12 December 1894.
A sailor who was hanged alongside Knight. He had shot his girlfriend, Sarah Jupe.

Philip Matthews – 21 July 1896.
Matthews worked for Teignmouth Council as a coachman and murdered his daughter because she was an encumbrance to his intended marriage. Matthews had met a young woman named Charlotte Mahoney and despite being already married, proposed to her. When Mrs Matthews discovered the affair she threw Matthews out, telling him to take his daughter with him. Matthews felt he could not tell his new lover about the child so strangled her in a woods.

Samuel Edward Smith – 21 July 1896.
A soldier in the King's Royal Rifles, based at Aldershot, Smith shot Corporal Payne after the latter had reported him.

Frederick Burden – 21 July 1896.
Chapter 3 in this volume.

Charles Maidment – 18 July 1899.
Chapter 4 in this volume.

William Churcher – 22 July 1902.
Churcher lived with his girlfriend, Sophia Jane Hepworth in Gosport. She had a drink problem and on the night of her death, Thursday, 10 April, was so under the influence that she fell into the river. During a subsequent argument over how she had embarrassed him in front of the neighbours, Churcher took out a knife and stabbed her in the throat and upper body. Her body was not discovered until two days later and in all, she had suffered thirty-three stab wounds. Sentenced to death by Mister Justice Bigham.

William Brown and Thomas Cowdrey – 16 December 1903. Hanged for the murder of a prostitute, Esther Atkins, near Aldershot, on Tuesday, 6 October. The two men were soldiers and had met Esther in the *Crimea* public house. Another man, John Dunbar, had also been accused of murder, but received a not guilty verdict. The trial, before Mister Justice Wills, lasted four days.

Augustus John Penny – 26 November 1913.
Chapter Five in this volume.

Walter James White – 16 June 1914.
Killed his girlfriend, Frances Priscilla Hunter at the *Goddard Arms Hotel*, in Swindon. White was devoted to Frances and marriage had been discussed but after a visit to members of Frances' family, White discovered that she had once lived with another man as his wife. Further, she had never told him of this fact. On Wednesday, 29 April, White visited the public house where Frances worked and shot her three times. He was sentenced to death by Mister Justice Ridley.

Leo George O'Donnell – 29 March 1917.
O'Donnell, a sergeant in the Royal Army Medical Corps, murdered his girlfriend's father, Lieutenant William Watterson at Aldershot, on Monday, 1 January. Watterson had been battered to death and one of the weapons used was a lavatory brush.

Thomas Henry Allaway – 19 August 1922.
One of the most curious cases of the twentieth century. On Wednesday, 1 December 1921, Allaway lured Irene May Wilkins from London to Bournemouth with the promise of a job and then battered her to death for no apparent reason. The subsequent investigation was badly bungled and although there were many opportunities to arrest him, Allaway managed to avoid detection until the following April. He was finally sentenced to death by Mister Justice Avory, after a five day trial.

Abraham Goldenberg – 30 July 1924.
Goldenberg, a serving soldier, robbed a branch of Lloyds Bank at Bordon and in the process, murdered the cashier William Edward Hall by shooting him, on Thursday, 3 April. Goldenberg was captured when Sergeant Major Thomas Alliott saw him hiding a parcel of money in a latrine.

Charles Edward Finden – 12 August 1926.
Murdered a fourteen-year-old schoolboy, John Richard Thompson, at Alton, on Saturday, 5 June, in order to steal his fifteen shillings wages from him.

William Henry Podmore – 22 April 1930.
Chapter 6 in this volume.

Sydney Archibald Frederick Chamberlain – 28 July 1949.
Although he was thirty-one years old, Chamberlain had a fifteen year old girlfriend, Doreen Primrose Messenger. On Saturday, 19 February, he took her on to Haldon Moor where he strangled her after they had talked about the difficulties of their relationship.

Roman Redel and Zbigniew Gower – 7 July 1950.
Two incompetent would-be bank robbers, who killed Robert Taylor at Bristol, when he tried to foil their getaway on Monday, 13 March. Redel and Gower, both Poles, had been drinking heavily the night before the planned robbery. As a result, they were unable to use the motorbike that had been intended and instead caught a bus to the scene of their crime. They managed to steal just £28 but failed to tie-up the bank clerk or guard with the result that they immediately raised the alarm. Trying to escape, again by bus, Robert Taylor, a judo expert, tried to stop them and was shot by Redel.

William Edward Shaughnessy – 9 May 1951.
Murdered his wife, Marie on Monday, 18 December 1950 and their daughter, Joyce, on the following day, at 319 Arundel Street, Portsmouth. Sentenced to death by Mister Justice Byrne.

Michael George Tatum – 14 May 1959.
Chapter 8 in this volume.

Dennis John Whitty – 17 December 1963.
Whitty and his partner in crime, Russell Pascoe, had heard that William Garfield Rowe had money hidden about his isolated home, Nanjarrow Farm at Constantine, near Falmouth. During the subsequent robbery, on Wednesday, 14 August, they murdered Rowe but missed most of the money. Both men were sentenced to death by Mister Justice Thesiger, after a five day trial. Whitty was hanged at Winchester and, at the same time, Pascoe was hanged at Bristol.

Index